EXPLORING
THE OUTDOORS WITH
INDIAN SECRETS

EXPLORING THE OUTDOORS WITH
INDIAN SECRETS

Allan F. Macfarlan

Stackpole Books

Copyright © 1971 by
Allan A. Macfarlan

Published by
STACKPOLE BOOKS
5067 Ritter Road
Mechanicsburg, PA 17055
www.stackpolebooks.com

with many illustrations by Paulette Macfarland
cover photograph by Barbara Hendershot

Printed in the U.S.A.

Library of Congress Cataloging in Publication Data

Macfarlan, Allan A.
  Exploring the outdoors with Indian secrets.

  Reprint. Originally published: Modern hunting
with Indian secrets. Harrisburg, Pa.: Stackpole
Books, 1971.
  1. Hunting.   2. Indians of North America—
Hunting.   3. Tracking and trailing.   I. Title.
SK33.M23   1982   799.2   82-5466
ISBN 0-8117-2183-3 (pbk.)   AACR2

Contents

8 INDIAN TRICKS FOR TAKING PREDATORS

The Wolverine
The Bobcat
- hunting with hounds • best times to call

The Big American Cats
- the cougar • the jaguar

9 GETTING CLOSE TO BIG GAME 183

The Buffalo
- how Indians drove buffalo on horseback
- hunting on game preserves

The Pronghorn Antelope
- the pronghorn's signaling system • the pronghorn's senses • how fast is the antelope? • hunting with gaze hounds • an Indian ruse for taking antelope • the Indian encirclement technique • modern methods of standing • modern methods of stalking

Elk
- finding the herd • elk whistles • typical elk terrain • range

Moose
- calling with a birchbark horn • using binoculars • why the moose is dangerous

Caribou
- Indian and Eskimo drives • locating and stalking a trophy animal
- Indian trick for getting within range

Mule and Columbia Blacktail Deer
- distinguishing the mule deer from the whitetail • capitalizing on the mule deer's curiosity • identifying the Columbia blacktail • range of the Columbia blacktail

The Black Bear
- range • weight • color variations • hunting methods of the Woodland Indians • dangers to man • tree-climbing ability
- how males stake out their territory • Indian methods of baiting
- hunting with hounds

The Grizzly Bear
- hunting vaquero-style with lariats and lances • hunting with bow and arrow

Spotting and Stalking the Alaska Brown Bear
The Polar Bear
Mountain Sheep and Mountain Goats
- Rocky Mountain bighorn sheep • desert bighorn sheep • stone sheep • Dall sheep • stalking mountain sheep • hunting sheep with bow and arrow • how to get a mountain goat trophy

Introduction

KNOWING THE WAYS in which Indians met the many challenges of the unknown will help the modern outdoorsman or woman to meet similar situations in field and forest. The chance to acquire and develop new skills lies in wait in the pages of this how-to book for those who will follow the well-marked trails which lead to adventure in the great outdoors.

In *Exploring the Outdoors with Indian Secrets,* the skills and techniques of the Indians are drawn from tribes whose vast hunting grounds used to cover the territory which is now the United States and Canada. The Indian was endowed with many natural qualities — keen eyes, sharp ears, an acute sense of smell, curiosity, and the ability to move stealthily, swiftly, and silently, seeing but unseen — and these were combined with courage, poise, patience, and stoicism. He developed and used these traits which were then and still are the secrets of success of a true hunter.

Exploring the Outdoors with Indian Secrets is written for hunters, fishermen, outdoorsmen, campers, photographers, hikers, and lovers of nature, since many of the pointers set down tell how to get the most out of outdoor living and how to become aware of what goes on in nature's domain.

A hunter may be proud of some exceptional trophy of the chase, but a fine photograph of animal life, taken at close quarters, is also a special prize which testifies to the photographer's ability and patience as a stalker; and nature lovers will cherish the vivid memory of meeting a wild creature face to face in the fastness of a forest.

Exploring the Outdoors with Indian Secrets has many descriptive drawings to illustrate the how-to and spur on the let's-do in the projects set down in its pages, and is a source book as well as an invitation and challenge to adventure for all who cherish the great outdoors and live with the glow of adventuring in their hearts.

1 /

Primitive Methods and The Modern Outdoorsman

WHO CAN PROFIT by learning the outdoor skills of the American Indian? Obviously, the modern hunter, but the outdoor photographer, beginning birdwatcher, and casual nature observer can benefit greatly too. All these outdoorsmen want to find birds or game and approach them silently and unobserved to close range. The hunter who uses short-range weapons—bow and arrow, shotgun, or muzzleloader—must be very close to his quarry before he flushes the bird and fires or pulls down on that vanishing buck. Even the long-range rifleman, who prides himself on his ability to pick off his mule deer or antelope at 300 yards or more can learn something from the Indians too—how to find game in the first place, for instance. And it's not always possible to find game out in the open. Even in the West, the skilled long-range shooter with his scoped .300 Magnum rifle sometimes finds himself tracking a buck into thick cover where the longest possible shot would be fired at no more than 50 yards.

THE INDIAN AS CLOSE-RANGE HUNTER

The Indian was a superb close-range hunter. His bows and arrows were crudely made short-range weapons, and throwing sticks and spears were used at very short range. The Indian's substitute for long-range killing was great skill at silent stalking and tracking and an ability to conceal himself when waiting for game. Even after the Indian acquired the white man's firearms, he did not use them well. In spite of legends to the contrary, most Indians were abominable shots with the early fifth-rate trade muskets, and even when they acquired fairly accurate rifles, they did not shoot well at long range. They did not need to do so.

Indians were notorious for abusing firearms. They often shot gravel or pebbles from rifled weapons. After a few charges of such "shot," the muzzleloading rifle became an inaccurate smoothbore. Front and rear sights seldom stayed in alignment with the bore of the gun after an Indian hunter had used it for a while. Their very carelessness with firearms demonstrates that Indians were not interested in long-range shooting.

When firearms came along, the Indian hunter was glad to adopt them because they killed more surely than his primitive weapons. A buffalo shot through the shoulders with a .50-caliber Sharps usually dropped in his tracks or ran only a few yards because of the shocking power of the heavy bullet. With a .44 rifle, a moose or elk could be knocked off his feet at close range, and then there was no difficult and dangerous job of tracking the animal through thick brush, perhaps in darkness. Hit with an arrow, even in a vital organ, a heavy animal sometimes ran a considerable distance or got away entirely. Modern bowhunters know that their shafts must be carefully placed when deer hunting because the arrow kills through hemorrhage, not through shock and large-scale destruction of animal tissue. To the Indian, a gun was a means of knocking the game animal down for keeps at close range. The Indian hunter quickly learned to use the muzzleloader with a shot charge to take several birds with a single shot while they were on the ground or perched along a branch. This too was a vast improvement over the bow and arrow.

TODAY'S NEED FOR
CLOSE-RANGE HUNTING SKILLS

Though the Indian hunter used firearms, he remained a close-range stalker of game, and many hunters today are finding that they must acquire the ability to get within close range of game. Many local governments and even a few entire states in thickly settled parts of the country prohibit hunting with rifles. On Long Island, New York, for instance, hunters must use shotguns. A rifle is too dangerous because of its long-range killing ability and its high velocity, which will put bullets through the average barn or wooden-frame house. In New Jersey, the use of rifles for anything except woodchuck hunting is forbidden by law. In that state, deer hunters must use a shotgun loaded with buckshot during the regular season or archery tackle during the bowhunting season. The New Jersey deer hunter finds himself in the same situation as the Indian hunter armed with bow and arrow or a smoothbore trade musket loaded with shot. In some counties close to large cities, the use of firearms for hunting is prohibited and the hunter must use bow and arrow. As population becomes more dense in many parts of the country, similar restrictions will undoubtedly be enacted by more and more townships, counties, and states. In some areas, one will either hunt like an Indian, or won't hunt at all. But it is also true that many hunters prefer primitive weapons, and are now using muzzleloading firearms loaded with ball or buckshot and black powder, and many hunters enjoy the challenge of hunting with bow and arrow.

In spite of his telescopic lenses, the outdoor photographer must often approach his "target" closely, and the same is true of the birdwatcher, who delights in identifying the many different forms of what Roger Tory Peterson calls "the confusing fall warblers." There are many species and subspecies of birds in the United States, and even with very good binoculars, one must be very close to differentiate among them. The birdwatcher must get closer than the shotgunner because the great prize of the birding enthusiast is the small bird, not the large one. It's easy to identify an eagle, but wrens present a problem. To be able to tell one species of warbler from another is much more difficult than identifying any game bird. The game birds are much larger, and the birdwatcher doesn't use dogs to scent them and point.

Many people do not hunt, do not take wildlife photographs, and are not interested in birdwatching. They just like to understand what they see on camping trips or hikes or during a walk in farm country. To do so, they must train their eyes to see what there is to see and their ears to identify what they hear.

It is difficult for some people to acquire the physical skills of the Indian hunter. A good Indian guide can spot a mountain sheep with the naked eye whereas a white man from the city finds it difficult to locate a whole band of them with field glasses. There are too many sheep-shaped rocks on the mountainside. The guide knows what to look for—small movements in particular—and he understands the sheep and knows where they are likely to be found at any time of day and where they go as a result of changing weather. It takes time, effort, and experience to acquire that kind of knowledge about every important game animal, and if you include birds and small mammals, it takes a lifetime.

INDIAN ENDURANCE

It would also be difficult for many of us to acquire the Indian hunter's outdoor endurance, and few of us would want to. The primitive Indian's spartan way of life shortened his life span, and few weaklings survived. Those who did survive were superb outdoorsmen. Even today, Indians and Eskimos in tribal groups that still live mainly by hunting and trapping have shorter life spans than those of average well-sheltered white men.

Most modern hunters wear heavy boots because they cannot endure the cold, the damp, and the thorns. But wearing heavy boots has a price. If you wear them, you make a great deal more noise than someone who goes barefoot or wears soft footwear. In this, a few modern hunters compromise. They wear heavy footgear when going long distances to or from a hunting area. If possible, though, they change to soft shoes when hunting.

Most people will find that hunting or observing nature by taking advantage of the Indian hunter's skills involves many compromises. For instance, most sheep and mountain-goat hunters use binoculars and a spotting scope to locate their game. It's impossible for most of us to do otherwise. But the modern hunter can learn where and how to spot the sheep or mountain goat—something the Indian hunter knew long before glass lenses were invented. In order to achieve what the Indian hunter accomplished through stamina, most of us must use modern equipment to supplement limited outdoor abilities and endurance. For instance, we substitute warm, waterproof clothing for the

Indian's stoical endurance, and there is nothing wrong in that. The Seminole endures the hideous insects of the Florida Everglades with fortitude. Most of us would go crazy without insect repellent.

INDIAN STRATAGEMS FOR SURVIVAL

Nowadays if you took game like an Indian, you would be arrested, imprisoned, or fined if you used some of his techniques. The Indian hunter wasn't a sportsman. Though he enjoyed hunting, he took game in the easiest way whenever possible because he hunted to eat and to obtain hides and furs. This was also true of the frontiersman and early settler. "Ground sluicing" birds with a shotgun and similar methods did not become unsportsmanlike in many areas until after the First World War. When you take game in order to stay alive, you are more interested in six quail dead on the ground with one charge of shot than you are in a single bird picked skillfully out of the sky, and ammunition was almost always in scarce supply among Indians and frontiersmen.

The Indian took much game and fish by using methods that are illegal today. For instance, many Great Lakes tribes hunted deer by "jacking" them at night. A fire was built on a flat stone in the bow of a canoe and some kind of upright shield was placed behind it. The hunter crouched behind the shield so he would not be temporarily blinded by the glare. The canoe was paddled by a squaw or a boy, and it moved silently along the shoreline until they found a deer, and the animal stood motionless, fascinated by the light. The shot was taken almost always at no more than ten or twelve yards. Frontiersmen and farmers imitated the Indian, but they used bull's-eye lanterns and a smoothbore musket or shotgun loaded with a charge of large shot. Today, the law in every American jurisdiction forbids hunting deer by jacklighting. Nevertheless, deer jacking was employed by the Indians, and it was therefore an Indian hunting method—before the white man began to do the same.

The Indians often used grain as bait to lure birds within range of throwing sticks and nets, and they often snared small game animals and birds. Most states forbid baiting for birds and game animals, and snares for trapping have been largely outlawed even for the licensed trapper because the snare is less efficient than a modern steel trap. Too many animals caught in snares manage to get away injured only to die later—a complete waste.

Nevertheless, it's wise to know something about jacking, baiting, snares, and other Indian techniques of this kind. The reason for this is indicated in the present-day game laws of the state of Alaska, subsection 81:370: "Nothing in these regulations prohibits a person from taking game, except migratory birds, for food during the closed season in case of dire emergency, nor do they prohibit taking of game in defense of life or property." If you are starving to death or defending yourself against a dangerous animal, Alaska does not prohibit your saving your life by killing a bird or animal even if the act violates closed-season regulations. Alaskan law-enforcement authorities are also understanding if a starving man uses an illegal weapon or trapping device to kill a game animal in order to save his own life. A starving man could not be expected to do otherwise. The reason why migratory game birds (primarily waterfowl) are excluded from the Alaska regulation is that laws controlling hunting for them are made and enforced by the federal government, which does not see fit to make this exception, perhaps because most of the officials in charge live in Washington, D.C., with a well-stocked grocery store nearby.

A number of American states had similar regulations. They have been gradually dropped for the most part because too many dishonest persons took advantage of them. It seems that a deer killed out of season was always destroying crops. A bear dropped out of season was always said to have been breaking into the smokehouse.

Even in the absence of a specific regulation allowing emergency kills, most game wardens, justices of the peace, and judges make due allowance for the man who kills game illegally because he is starving or in self-defense. The Alaska regulation goes on to require prompt reporting of any illegal kill to a game warden, and the hunter is not allowed to keep any trophy from the kill. Even in other states, it's always wise to report involuntary violations of the game laws. If you can satisfy a game warden that you killed illegally only to stave off starvation or in order to protect yourself, it's unlikely that you will be prosecuted. If the law is enforced, it's better to pay a fine or go to jail than it is to starve to death or be bitten by a rabid fox.

More and more photographers, campers, nature observers, and nonresident hunters are venturing into wilderness areas where they sometimes find themselves in a situation in which a minor game infraction would save them. In the deer woods of the Upper Peninsula of Michigan, for instance, it's possible to wander for many days without crossing a road or seeing another person. Many hunters and outdoorsmen have done so, and a number of them ended their ordeals in death. In some of these cases, the lost person could have survived if he had known how to set an illegal snare or how to catch even a songbird to eat. Many campers, birdwatchers, and nature photographers seldom think of killing animals or birds. Therefore, they do not know how to do so, and it has cost some of them their lives. Knowing about a few of the illegal Indian methods of taking game and fish might save your life someday.

It's also true that in most states and Canadian provinces, many birds, animals, and fish are not on the protected list and may be taken by any means at any time—without a license in many jurisdictions. In most states that have them, for instance, the woodchuck, the prairie dog, the red squirrel, and the coyote are "varmints," and they are open all year round to all comers. The rattlesnake is fair game at all times everywhere, and can be eaten, as many tribesmen knew. Even a rattlesnake that has been bitten by another is edible, provided the consumer does not have a loose tooth, wound, or sore in his mouth where the venom could enter his bloodstream. Some people would starve to death rather than eat a rattlesnake because of their mistaken impression that the snake's flesh is poisonous.

Not very appetizing fare, perhaps, but if you're starving, you'll even set traps for mice, as many Indians did when their regular game failed. You have to know how to do it, though, and this book contains a drawing of an Indian mousetrap used to take the tiny animals for food.

Starvation sometimes did stalk the tribes. When the snowshoe hares declined in the Northeast due to regular cycles of disease that occurred and still occur about every seven years, the Canada lynx that preyed upon them died off. The tribal hunter was just as much a predator on the hare as the lynx was, and when the big hares died off, his people declined too. This was particularly true when the cycle occurred for hares and grouse at the same time. Only those who could find and kill the scarce remaining hares and grouse or who could locate and take other game survived. When the deer moved out of the tribal hunting grounds because some accident of nature reduced their browse, the Indian who depended on deer starved unless he could locate other game or move with the deer.

Hunting and fishing is a precarious way of life. Only those tribes and individual hunters who developed skill in taking game animals, birds, and fish survived. The early settlers marveled at the skill and endurance of the Indian hunter and trapper. Some of us still do not realize that only the very skilled and those capable of great endurance stayed alive in any hunting-and-fishing culture—a good example of "survival of the fittest."

Since only the fittest survived in the harsh northern cultures, the white man seldom encountered an unskilled Indian hunter. Few modern Americans would care to undergo the hardships that the Indian endured in order to learn his outdoor skills and develop his endurance. We can, however, learn much that is useful from the Indian's harsh experience.

2 /

Game-catching with Traps and Snares

INDIANS AND EARLY frontiersmen took fish in every possible way because they needed vast quantities for food and fertilizer. Trapping was also important as a means of securing food and skins. The frontiersman and the Indian preferred to use a net, trap, or snare because that did not use up scarce powder and lead.

Only a few primitive methods of taking fish and game are described here, but they give a good idea of the techniques that were used. Any outdoorsman can develop variations that will work well with the kind of fish or game he is trying to harvest. As pointed out earlier, however, many of these methods are illegal and should not be used unless you are in danger of starvation.

INDIAN WAYS TO CAPTURE FISH

Weirs

One way to catch fish wholesale was to use a weir made of saplings, brushwood, or netting. Usually, poles and brush were shoved into the bottom of a river, stream, channel, or saltwater inlet. The current or tide swept the fish down into the weir, and long wings or a slanted

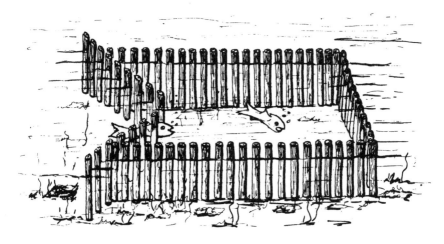

Fish Weir

construction guided the fish into a tight enclosure from which they could not escape. Even today, one or two weirs built entirely of brush are still in use on the shore of the Bay of Fundy, and eel weirs are still in operation in the Delaware River. A small fish weir built of brush can be thrown across a stream in an emergency and a basket woven of bark can be mounted at a narrow opening in its center. If you then go upstream and splash as you come downstream, it's likely that you'll drive at least a few fish into the basket or other trap in the weir. Sometimes, a simple V-shaped barrier of stones or brush, open end upstream, is effective.

Spearing

The Indians of the Northwest Coast often built platforms of various sorts for fish spearing on rocks in fast-flowing salmon streams. They also placed them in overhanging trees and on the banks of streams. The target was the salmon migrating upstream to spawn. The Indian fishermen speared thousands of the huge fish from these platforms and threw them up onto the bank where women kept fires burning and set up great racks on which to smoke them. For a starving man on a salmon stream, one of these fine fish attempting to jump a waterfall or rapids is an easy target. They can be taken with a gaff or a dip net with a long handle. The trick is to be where the salmon will again hit the water after a leap with your spear or net ready. There is a moment when the fish hits the surface in which it is fairly still and can be taken easily. Fish also rest in quiet spots behind rocks before jumping. At those points, the Indians located spearing and netting platforms.

The drawing shows a simple head for a fish spear that is easily carved out of hardwood or springy bone with a sheath knife. A triangular piece of wood keeps the two halves separate under the binding that holds them together. The head must be mounted on a shaft. The end of the shaft can also be shaped to keep the prongs apart. From above, the head is thrust down upon the fish, and if the spearman is lucky, it will lodge around the fish's body.

Trotlines

Indian fishermen used trotlines long before the first white men came to this hemisphere. A trotline, called a set line when it is used in salt

Fish Spear Head

water, consists of one main line with many short "warps" or "droppers" hanging down from it, each one with a hook. The Indians rigged trotlines across streams, rivers, and saltwater inlets. If a narrow body of water was very productive, a trotline was often strung down its center. The Indians used strong, woven-fiber main lines and thinner, but very strong, dropper lines. The dropper lines or warps were tied onto the main line three or four feet apart according to the water being fished. Very strong gear was needed in some cases because many large fish might be hooked on a single trotline. Even today, trotlines are still in use in the American South, particularly when fishing commercially for catfish. In the Maritime Provinces of Canada, hardy dorymen still launch from the beach and put out set lines for cod, pollock, and haddock. Whenever possible, a boat is used to take fish from the lines. One man paddles or poles the boat along the trotline. Another lifts the long line and takes the fish off. When the catch does not weigh too much, trotlines are often pulled in from the shore. Sometimes, one or two men can wade along a line and remove the fish one by one as they lift the long line. It's dangerous if the fish are large and the line is slack. If a big catfish suddenly jerks on the line, for instance, he may drive an empty hook into your hand or arm and pull you underwater, and it's even more dangerous if the commotion causes other fish farther along the line to rise from the bottom and try to swim off.

Dip Nets

The Indians caught many fish in cone-shaped wicker fish traps of varying sizes. They also used dip nets and other nets made from fiber netting or animal hides. Some nets were shaped like potato sacks. Others were made from large oblong pieces of hide with the hair scraped off. The skins were made into nets by punching or cutting many holes through them, and several hides could be sewn together to make a large net. The same thing can be done with heavy, strongly woven canvas. Handles were provided on each end and two men stretched the net between them. Knowing that fish idle and feed with their heads pointing upstream, the netters worked against the current toward some obstacle such as a waterfall beyond which the fish could not swim. As they moved upstream, they took time to net worthwhile fish from pools and shallows. They continued upstream until they reached the obstacle, where the remaining fish were taken with the net.

Gill Nets

In large bodies of water where the fish were not confined between banks, gill nets were often most effective. The meshes of these nets were made just large enough to admit the heads of the fish and pass over their gills. Most often, the fish was firmly held as soon as the mesh passed the gills because it was then caught on the dorsal fin or the widest part of the fish's body. If the fish struggled backwards, the net caught in its flaring gills. A long curtain of gill net suspended on buoys is still one of the most popular ways to net large quantities of fish, particularly herring and salmon. It's very important to make the squares of the net the exact size to catch the average fish in the school. Hook-and-line fishing in strange waters usually tells the fisherman how large his meshes should be. Even a crudely woven small net strung between two poles or suspended from floats will take enough fish to keep a man alive if there are any fish at all in the water and the net is set so that it forms a curtain from surface to bottom in fairly shallow water. In deeper water, only topwater fish can be taken with a gill net because the net usually cannot be made deep enough to reach the depth where bottom fish such as catfish and suckers are found.

Nooses

Suckers and several other varieties that do not readily take baited hooks were often caught in clear streams and ponds by means of a thin, strong noose made of hide. It was fastened to the end of a light pole. The noose was skillfully passed over the head of a big sucker or other large fish. As soon as the noose reached a point just behind the gills, the pole was yanked, and the fish was thrown up onto the bank. This method is still used by farm boys to catch rough fish such as the redhorse and the buffalofish, but thin copper bell wire, stripped of insulation is used for the noose instead of leather. The wire is stiff enough to hold the noose open until the pole is jerked. A coil of thin copper wire is a very good item to put into a survival kit. It can be used for noosing fish, and it also makes excellent snares for small game such as rabbits.

The hardy Yuki fishermen of California often went after fish by diving into the water. They also caught fine salmon by slipping running nooses over their tails.

Lines, Hooks, and Lures

Many Indian fishermen used a willow pole, sinew fishing line, and composite hooks made of wood and bone or wood and a piece of shell. The shank of the hook was usually made of wood, but the curved part and the barb, if any, was made of bone or shell. The two parts were carefully lashed together.

Attractive artificial lures made from wood and stone were used effectively on the Northwest Coast by Indian fishermen. Good lures of various sizes were often made from lightweight wood cut and colored

Indian Fishhooks

to represent fish. Trolled behind a boat, these lures decoyed big fish to the surface, where they were speared.

A very simple form of hook was made from a pencillike length of hardwood sharpened at both ends. The line was tied around a groove in its middle. This primitive hook was run lengthwise through a dead minnow or herring. When a fish swallowed the bait, the fisherman jerked hard on the line, causing the two pointed ends of the wooden rod to penetrate the sides of its mouth or throat. This type of hook is easy to make and could be useful in an emergency.

The Haida used fine, strong fish lines made from thin strips of redcedar bark or kelp. When new, these lines were flexed and rubbed to make them supple. These tribesmen also made a strange lure from wood and other materials that looked like the feathered shuttlecock used in badminton. This lure was pushed deep under the water with a long pole. When released, it twirled slowly to the surface. It was often followed by one or more big fish which were speared.

INDIAN TRAPS FOR BIG AND SMALL GAME

Indian trappers used many different kinds of animal and bird traps. Even large animals such as elk, deer, bear, and bighorn sheep were trapped with various devices built to suit the circumstances and terrain. Traps were made for smaller animals such as the wolf, coyote, fisher, fox, marmot, woodchuck, wolverine, badger, jackrabbit, and cottontail. The Indians also used traps for small animals such as ground squirrels, tree squirrels, chipmunks, weasels, rats, and mice. These small traps were set by the youngsters of the villages and encampments, who were learning the rudiments of trapping at an early age, or by adults when food was scarce.

How to make and operate certain efficient traps was known by widely scattered tribes because such information was quickly circulated by traveling traders, hunters, and trappers. These traps were supplemented by many more of original and ingenious construction that best met conditions in each tribe's area. All the earlier traps and nets were made of twigs, trees, branches, logs, withes, rawhide thongs, human and animal hair, roots, and natural fibers. No metals were used in spite of the fact that some tribes knew how to smelt and work copper.

The biggest traps took the form of huge pounds or corrals (for buffalo), stockades, pens, and cages of many sorts into which the game was driven or lured with bait. The Indians also used traps in the form of boxes; deadfalls; pits, trenches, holes in the ground; hooks; and nooses. Their trapping devices were released by triggers, latches, thongs, or the hidden trapper, waiting in a blind nearby. Among the most effective traps were those that were sprung by the animals themselves. These traps and snares were released by pulling, friction, gnawing, or the animal's manipulation, caused by curiosity.

Deadfalls

For bear and wolverine, and some other game, deadfalls were used. In its simplest form, the trapper merely propped a heavy log on a heavy trigger stick and tied the bait onto the trigger. Sometimes two short sticks were driven into the ground, one on each side, to hold the heavy log on the trigger stick. Any deadfall, and most other traps, are more effective when an enclosure is built to guide the animal into position. Sometimes sticks were driven into the ground, but often rough lines of cut brush on both sides were used.

An improvement on the simple deadfall is shown in the drawing of the figure-4 trap. The figure-4 trap or deadfall is easy to make, but the size of the falling log and the trigger sticks must be carefully chosen to suit the size of the quarry. This trap was and is used to take everything from small birds to bears. For birds and small mammals, the Indians used a box or a cage balanced on the stick labeled A. One end of the box or cage rested on the ground, and the other end rested on the stick. For larger animals, stronger trigger sticks were used and the deadfall was a heavy log that fell on the trapped animal and killed it outright.

For big game, the trappers usually arranged the deadfall so that the log fell on the head or neck of the animal. This was accomplished by putting up a tight wall of cut brush or sticks shoved into the ground on one side of the trap so that the animal could not approach from that side or from the end of the trap where the trigger stick was set up, the brush or sticks being curved around the trigger arrangement to prevent entry. When the animal approached the open side, it had to reach the bait by putting its head well under the deadfall. Sometimes a

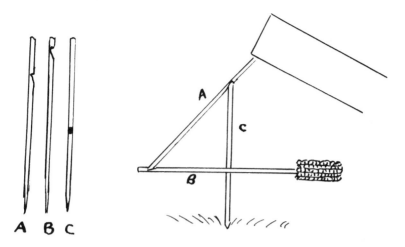

Figure-4 Deadfall

curving object such as a fallen log or a rocky wall or bank could be used to guide the animal into the trap. Trappers who wanted to make sure of their quarry often built a small stockade of logs around the entire trap so that the animal could not escape the deadfall by streaking out from under it. A narrow entrance angled the animal into the trap so that backing out was a slow process.

The notches in the trigger sticks must be cleanly cut and the wood for the sticks should be firm and strong. They can be hardwood cut in a home workshop or straight branches cut and shaped in the forest. The box or weight is balanced delicately on the trigger sticks when feel tells the trapper that they can support the weight. Setting this trap is not as easy as the drawing suggests. When the C-stick is slightly sharpened at the ground end, it may be thrust a little way into the earth, but too much depth makes the trap more difficult to spring when the quarry comes along. If possible, a blunt-ended stick merely placed on flat, firm ground helps to collapse the whole trigger arrangement when the animal takes the bait or merely touches it. It's a matter of practice until the trapper develops the needed skill. Setting any trap built of wood or other natural materials is a tricky job. Each trap is necessarily slightly different, and the trapper has to develop a feel for it. The tension of modern steel traps and the trigger action is determined in advance by the manufacturer.

Most trappers who use modern traps fasten the trap chain to a heavy object such as a length of heavy branch or light log which is used as a drag. The trapped animal pulls the drag after him each time he tries to pull out of the trap. Though it may drag the weight a fair distance, the animal cannot go far enough to escape if the trapper has been wise enough to choose a drag of the right weight. It is easy to follow the scrape marks left by the dragging weight in snow, on the ground, in pine needles, or in fallen leaves. The drag turns leaves or needles up, and their damp undersides show a plain trail.

Foxes, coyotes, badgers, and coons were often caught in a deadfall set inside a long narrow cubby built of poles driven into the ground. This type of deadfall was often used when the trapper found it difficult to cut or set up the figure-4 trigger sticks. Two tall poles about eight feet long were placed at the extreme ends of the cubby or stockade, which had only one entrance. The long, narrow cubby forced the animal to stand lengthwise under the deadfall, which was a piece of heavy hardwood log two or three feet long and at least one foot in diameter. A stout rawhide thong was tightly strung between the tops of the tall end poles, and the deadfall log was suspended from it by another thong tied with a slipknot that was carefully arranged to release the deadfall at the slightest tug. Grease on the thong where the knot was tied insured easy release. Sometimes one end of the log rested on the ground; sometimes it was easier to drive long withes into the ground to keep the deadfall suspended lengthwise over the cubby. A piece of tough, raw meat was tied securely to the bottom of the suspended log. When the animal entered the trap and pulled on the bait, the slipknot did its work and the log fell on the animal and killed it. As with other primitive traps, the arrangement must be varied to suit the size and habits of the quarry, the trap-building materials that are available, and the terrain and vegetation where the trap is used.

Rawhide Nooses

Though deer, elk, and caribou were often driven into stockades, which were used over and over again, the usual way to take these animals was with strong rawhide or sinew nooses. These were spread open in a deer trail or concealed in vegetation where the animals were known to feed regularly. The stiffness of the rawhide helped to hold the noose wide open so that it would pass over the animal's head. It then pulled tight as the animal tried to move on, often strangling the quarry before the trapper arrived. The noose was much more likely to pass entirely over the head of doe deer and cow elk since there were no antlers, but a buck caught securely by his rack seldom escaped. Approaching an antlered animal in a snare or other trap is dangerous. The trapped animal can strike swiftly with its sharp front hoofs, and the antler points can be dangerous too, though most antlered animals use their feet against human enemies.

The free end of the line in which the noose was formed was often fastened to the supple upper end of a small but tough sapling. This provided a springy anchor which served the same purpose as the drag or clog that is now attached to modern steel traps. Since the anchor was springy, there was much less chance for the animal to snap the thong.

Bent-Branch Snare

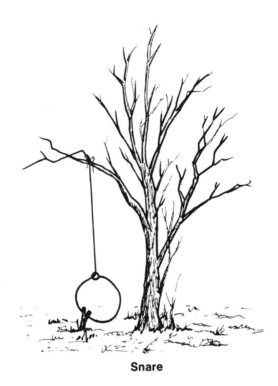

Snare

Strong but flexible wire makes a good substitute for rawhide when making a snare. If rawhide or wire is too flexible to stay open, tie the slip loop open with weak material such as grass or slender withes attached to suitable surrounding vegetation. Snares are effective with some of the smaller game animals such as cottontail rabbits that often use well-established runways where the snares can be set.

Pits

The Cree, among the finest Indian trappers, caught wolves and foxes in cleverly constructed and concealed pits. They were fitted with a revolving trap door. The door was baited with tough, raw meat securely fastened on top. When a wolf tried to take the bait, the animal's weight revolved the pivoted door so that it turned rightside up again. The wolf dropped into the deep pit, but the baited door remained in position for the next wolf. Sometimes half a dozen animals were trapped in the same pit. This same trap, built on a smaller scale, can be used for foxes and coyotes.

Ingenious Ways for Taking Wolves

Blackfoot Indian trappers sometimes built great circular traps that caught as many as fifty wolves in one night. These were made by driving stout stakes closely together in a big circle. The stakes were driven into the ground at an angle of about forty-five degrees, inclining toward the center of the circle. Earth was placed against the stakes outside the enclosure at one point to form a ramp. Part of a dead buffalo or some other carcass was placed on the ground inside the enclosure. When wolves climbed the ramp and jumped down inside, it was impossible for them to jump out again because of the height of the stakes and their inward angle.

Some northern Indians learned a cruel but effective method of killing wolves from the Eskimos. A strip of springy whalebone or a thin, long fishbone was sharpened at each end. The springy bone was bent into a circle with the ends overlapping, and a thong was used to tie the ends together. The circle of springy bone was then encased in blubber or fat and left outside in the extreme cold until the fat froze. The fat was then slit with a knife to remove the thong from the overlapped ends, and more fat was added and frozen to conceal the slit. The ball of frozen fat was left lying where tracks showed that a wolf might soon find it. When the animal swallowed the ball whole because it was too hard to chew, the animal's body heat thawed the fat, and the pointed ends sprang straight. The ends pierced the animal's stomach walls, and the animal died in agony. Using larger, longer bones and a large ball of fat, this method was often used for bear, and it also worked with wolverine. The trick was to make the ball just the right size for the animal to swallow easily.

Traps for Small Rodents

The accompanying drawing shows a trap for very small animals such as mice, rats, and chipmunks, all of which are excellent food if a man is starving. It is made of wire mesh of varying sizes. The trap is baited with almost any kind of nut, grain, or waste food by dropping it through the funnel. The animals enter through the funneled end and cannot get out again because they cannot find the small end of the funnel, which must be an inch or more above the floor of the trap. The trapped animals are removed from the trap through a slit made in the end or at one side of the trap, which is then wired shut. The Indians built these traps out of thin hardwood splints or withes, but wire is better because the trapped animal cannot gnaw its way out of the trap.

This trap can also be used for minnows, either to eat or to use as bait. The best bait for this trap is bread or grain, but grubs and crushed shellfish sometimes work well. Weight the trap so that it will not roll away and use a buoy on a line to mark its location. Remove the minnows by opening the slit.

Because this trap is easily made and can be used for fish as well as small animals, a sheet of rolled-up wire screening is a useful piece of survival equipment. It occupies but little space in a survival kit.

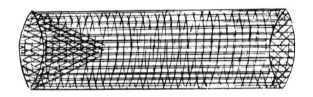

Indian-Style Mousetrap

WEAPONS AND RUSES FOR TAKING BIRDS

The Indians often trapped and hunted birds such as eagles, turkeys, hawks, and the large woodpeckers to obtain feathers for decoration and for fletching arrows. The feathers of the turkey, turkey buzzard, and the various geese were used a great deal for fletching.

Small birds were seldom taken with bow and arrow, though some young hunters took them with very light, pronged spears or with arrows with blunt points that killed or stunned by impact. Boys of the Plains tribes were taught to snare birds with nooses made of horsehair. The small nooses were tied about six inches apart on a stick that was placed on the ground. Seeds or grain were scattered as bait. Some birds nearly always got their legs entangled in these snares, and the watching boys ran from cover to kill them before they could escape. The stick to which the nooses were tied acted as a drag.

Quail

By studying the habits of quail, California Indians learned that the western forms of this game bird like to follow a low fence, natural hedge, or line of brush rather than fly over it. To trap the quail, they attached nooses made of fine thongs to bushes or branches at openings in the runways and also placed the nooses where the runways ended. Sometimes the Indians baited the ground near the nooses. From time to time, boys or women removed the birds caught in the snares, which were then reset.

Turkeys

An odd, simple trap was used to catch the wary wild turkey. Two poles were driven into the ground about ten feet apart. A much lighter pole was tied between the two uprights about fourteen inches above the ground. The trap was then baited with grains of maize. Knowing the habits of the birds, the Indians knew the direction of their approach and scattered corn under the length of the pole and six to twelve inches beyond it. A few women and boys then hid nearby and stayed quiet. When the turkeys reached the trap and began feeding on the grain, they soon had to stretch their necks beneath the crossbar to reach the grain. A wild turkey does not seem to be able to withdraw its head from under a low horizontal pole. The hidden trappers rushed from their blind and snatched the self-trapped birds.

Geese

Canada geese, snow geese, and blue geese were trapped in an equally simple way. A trench about eighteen feet long, eighteen inches deep, and fourteen inches wide was dug in the ground. Kernels of maize were sparingly scattered along the length of the trench, and the trench trap was ready. The trappers took cover close to the trap. When the geese flew in, they began to eat the grain at the ends of the trench, then continued into the trench itself in search of more corn. When several geese were in the trench, the trappers rushed from cover and seized the birds. The geese could not fly away because they did not have enough room to spread their wings in the narrow trench.

Magpies

Boys and young men who needed magpie feathers for decoration asked help from the wind. The ungainly tail of a magpie is very awkward on gusty days. When shaken out of their roost in tall bushes or low trees during windy weather, the birds flew so erratically that they were easily caught by hand.

Crows

It was a difficult feat to catch crows by hand, but it was done. The trappers hid in clumps of evergreens and covered themselves with branches to which tempting pieces of meat and fat were fastened with thin, strong thongs. When a crow landed on a baited branch, the bird was seized through the camouflaging branches. Crows came to these ambushes if the bait was used in an area where crows fed regularly; so calls were seldom used to bring them in. Magpies were also taken in this way. Some tribes in California flushed low-roosting crows at night and caught them in their confused flight by using fan-shaped nets.

Shown in the drawing is an effective live trap for crows and magpies. It could be used for other birds too. Though modern materials are used, it follows the general lines of several traps that were used by Indians. Trappers, farmers, and gun clubs have used this trap to advantage to eliminate the destructive birds.

This type of trap can be used to catch from ten to fifty or even more crows with one baiting, depending on the size of the trap. The trap is best made from old, weathered poles or saplings, carefully covered with 1½-inch, used wire mesh. It can also be made from finished lumber and new chicken wire, but it usually won't work well until the materials become weathered, since crows are alert, sus-

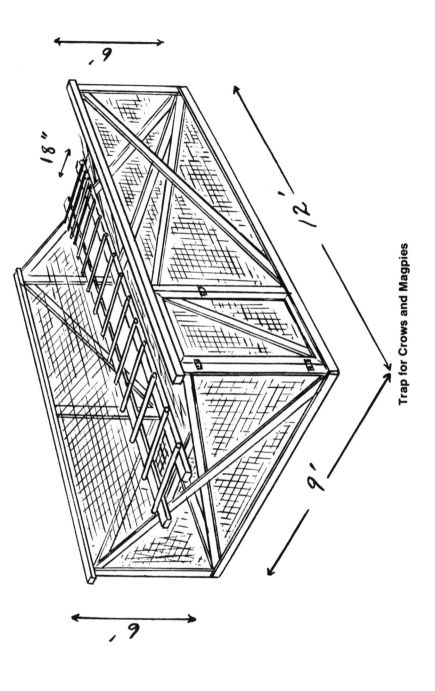

9'

9'

12'

18"

9'

Trap for Crows and Magpies

picious birds which often shy away from shiny, unnatural-looking objects. A door or small hatch should be made in one end of the trap so that it can be baited and emptied easily.

A horizontal ladder runs along the entire top of the trap. It is attached to the open, V-shaped top of the trap and forms the open roof through which the crows enter. The rungs of the ladder should be about ten inches apart. Though the crows enter the trap without difficulty by dropping through the ladder, they are unable to climb or fly out again. The open wings of the birds will not pass through the small openings between the rungs in the ladder.

The frenzied cries of a few trapped crows will bring more to the trap, most of which join those already inside. Since the first birds will eat up the bait, it is a good idea to leave a few crows in the trap all the time, since their cries act as the most effective bait. Pieces of raw meat or corn are good baits.

Trojan Horse Techniques
for Ambushing Waterfowl

Woodland Indians caught waterfowl in a unique way. A round wicker basket was woven from withes. A thong was fastened across the basket about halfway between the top and the bottom. Two or three slits were cut through the sides of the basket as peepholes. Armed with a few thin thongs with nooses in their ends, the trapper submerged at the shore of the lake. He swam silently toward the waterfowl with the basket over his head and shoulders, held down and controlled with the horizontal thong. The taut thong inside the basket was tucked under the trapper's chin or held between his teeth when he needed the free use of both hands.

The trapper swam slowly and silently toward the birds. The unsuspecting waterfowl were seldom alarmed by the basket floating on the surface. The hidden trapper seized two birds, one in each hand, by the legs from underneath. The most skillful trappers slipped a thong noose over the feet of a bird and went on to noose as many as four or five. The end of each line was attached to a peg driven into the shore. They swam ashore; then, tugging the ends of the thongs, they pulled the struggling birds ashore.

Some tribes used hollowed-out pumpkins instead of baskets. When the birds were wary, the Indians often left several empty pumpkins floating on the stream or pond. When the waterfowl became used to seeing the pumpkins, the trapper could approach them easily with a hollow pumpkin over his head.

The Déné Indians of the Northwest trapped many kinds of waterfowl by snaring them with thin thong nooses pegged out in shallow water. The Carrier Indians caught waterfowl by disguising themselves. They wore a headdress made of the head, neck, and forebody of a swan or goose which covered the trapper's head but allowed him to breathe. The trappers swam out toward the birds with thong nooses. The end of each long thong was fastened securely to a peg driven into the shore. When these trappers reached the feeding geese, ducks, or other waterfowl, they slipped nooses over the legs of as many birds as they could reach without disturbing the others. When all nooses were used, the trappers swam ashore and pulled in the birds.

Experienced trappers knew countless ruses and often planned large-scale trapping of waterfowl. When a tribal group decided to trap a large number of ducks feeding on a lake, they made use of the counsel of an elder who was wise in trapping and had participated in many mass trappings.

After the elder had studied the wind, water, and the habits of the wildfowl on the lake, he directed the operation. Huge nets were mounted on long, strong poles and set up on two sides of a square or in the form of a crescent the night before the trap was to be used. In the early morning when the waterfowl were feeding close to the nets, beaters rushed from the opposite shore and waded or swam toward the birds. Sometimes, canoes were used. When the startled ducks and other waterfowl took off, they flew directly into the nets. This type of trapping depended on expert placement of the nets, position of the flocks, and perfect timing.

TRAPS FOR SNAPPING TURTLES

When food was scarce, Indians hunted and trapped snapping turtles. Today, many people relish snapper cutlets and snapper soup. The common snapper sometimes weighs as much as 50 pounds. The alligator snapping turtle of the South often weighs as much as 100, and 200-pounders have been recorded. Both turtles have strong jaws and their bites can sever fingers or even a wrist. The common snapping turtle can strike with the swiftness of a snake.

The Indians also hunted land tortoises and took them in various simple traps and by hand. These land tortoises were often caught in the early morning when they came out of their burrows to drink the cool dew.

Shown in the drawing is a snapping-turtle trap which the author developed from Indian designs. This trap is built from modern materials, and several Indian groups now use this modernized version of ancient traps with great success.

Small Snapping-Turtle Trap

An old but strong wooden box three or four feet square and ten or more inches high, depending on the size of the turtles to be taken, is the basis of the trap. The wood should be about three-quarters of an inch thick. Drill a number of one-inch holes through the sides and bottom of the box to allow it to sink quickly and to let the water out of it when it is lifted.

The trap may also be made by covering a strong wooden frame with 1½-inch heavy wire mesh. That type is shown in the drawing. One end or side of the box or frame is hinged to form a door. The door should be made smaller than the frame so that the water will not swell the wood enough to jam it when closed. About one inch trimmed from one end and one side of a close-fitting door usually prevents jamming, but it is wise to soak the wood in water overnight before sawing the edges off to make sure that the door will not swell too much.

A block of hardwood nailed onto the frame of the floor of the trap at both corners or a narrow, thin strip of wood nailed across the bottom of the box, outside, prevents the door being pushed open from the inside by a trapped turtle. Once the doorstops are in place, hinge the door at the top with two strong, oiled-leather hinges, since metal hinges deteriorate too quickly. The door must be centered in the opening with the same clearance all around or it will not open smoothly. A screweye in each corner of the top of the box completes the trap. A short length of rope is tied to each screweye, and the ends of these lines are tied to a metal ring. The main handling line is also fastened to this ring. The trap can be weighted down with a few stones to keep it from floating, but it's convenient to nail on some heavy metal if it is available.

Raw meat, fishheads, or whole fish are placed inside the trap as bait. The trap is lowered to the bottom where snappers have been seen or where they have been caught on the hooks of trotliners or rod-and-reel fishermen. The free end of the main handling line is tied to a float or an overhanging branch. When the trap is left overnight, the catch is often surprising and may even include big fish.

Snappers should be grasped firmly about halfway down the shell, a hand on each side. The jaws cannot reach your hands that way, but you have to be careful to make sure that your hands are also out of reach of the sharp claws. A snapper cannot withdraw its head inside its shell; so some trappers like to slip a wire noose fastened to a stout pole around the snapper's neck and handle it that way. Keep your legs clear of the turtle's jaws and claws too.

A big trap, often used to take snappers on a large scale, is also illustrated. The logs used in the frame are about four feet long and eight inches in diameter. A wire basket about two feet deep made of old chicken wire hangs down from all four sides. The insides of the logs bordering the wire basket are covered with sheet metal to prevent the turtles crawling out of the trap.

The trap is set in water and anchored there. A wooden ramp leads from the water to the edge of the frame. The trap is baited with raw meat or fish. It is a good idea to wrap some of the bait in wire mesh

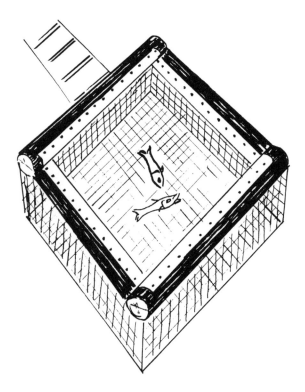

Large Snapping-Turtle Trap

so that the first snapper caught will not eat it all. Smelling the bait, snappers climb the ramp and drop into the trap. They cannot get out again because their claws cannot grip the sheet metal on the frame.

Remove the trapped snappers carefully by hand or with a strongly made dip net or wire noose on the end of a pole. Don't try to handle any big alligator snapper alone. They are very strong.

This trap can take almost all turtles in the water where the trap is set. A sportsman keeps only the snappers. Most other freshwater turtles are poor table fare, and are not destructive to fish or waterfowl.

3 /

Indian Ways to
Bowhunting Skills

MOST INDIAN BOWS were crudely fashioned. They were made in many different ways from many different woods and other materials. Some of the woods used for Indian bows were ash (a variety of American yew), second-growth hickory, Osage orange, dogwood, ironwood, mountain juniper, and cedar (sinew-wrapped). All early wooden bows were made from one solid piece of wood, but some Indians made fine bows from bone and horn. Some hunters discovered that bows were stronger and shot farther when they were tightly wrapped in the sinews of various animals. Rattlesnake skin was used for that purpose too.

TRIBAL ARCHERY GEAR

The Sioux and many other Indian horsemen used short bows about three feet six inches long because they were easier to handle on horseback. Many hunters shot arrows through both shoulders of a buffalo with these short but powerful weapons. Each hunter adjusted the pull of his bow to suit himself and the game he hunted. The length of the bows used by Indians on foot ranged from about four to six feet, depending on how and where the weapon was used. Tribes that hunted in brushy country did not favor long bows because it was hard to handle such weapons in a thicket. Usually, Indian archery tackle came into play at fairly short range. The Indian hunter depended on hunting skill, or horsemanship, to get close to the quarry rather than on accurate, powerful long-range tackle.

Many sorts of arrows were made by various tribes out of many different kinds of wood. The so-called arrowwood of the Indians was a variety of dogwood or viburnum. Some tribes used strong reeds and cane shoots for their shafts. The arrows varied in length from about twenty-four to thirty inches.

Points of many varying shapes were made from the tips of antlers, chipped stone, flaked stone, flint, and obsidian (a glassy volcanic rock).

Fletching

All the arrows of a tribe were often fletched with the wing feathers of the same kind of bird, usually a bird of prey such as the eagle, or a certain kind of hawk or owl, though some tribes preferred the wing feathers of the wild turkey. Fletching varied greatly. The Woodland tribes, for instance, fastened the feathers to the shaft in a spiral that differs entirely from the straight fletching of the Plains tribes. Fletching of this type was used by Indians who hunted in thick cover. Modern archers call it "flu-flu" fletching. Instead of the usual three vanes, as many as eight may be used, and the feathers are put on in a spiral pattern. The bushy, spiralled feathers permit the arrow to leave the bow and fly a short distance (twenty-five to thirty yards) at fairly high velocity. The drag of the flu-flu fletching keeps the head forward, the shaft following on a straight course. But at maximum range, the special fletching puts a brake on velocity, and the arrow drops quickly to the ground. Because of its short range, an arrow with flu-flu fletching is less likely to be lost after a miss.

Flu-flu fletching is most useful when hunting small game, especially when shooting birds and small mammals out of trees. For these elevated shots, an arrow with straight fletching will fly too far and be lost if it misses the game. The few bowhunters who try for winged game in flight prefer flu-flu fletching for the same reason—it stops their shafts after a short flight.

Flu-flu fletching is often used with rounded, blunt-pointed arrows that kill the game by impact rather than penetration and blood loss. A small animal such as a squirrel, hit with a broadheaded hunting arrow, is so mutilated that much of the meat is spoiled. Just as the Indians did before them, some modern archers go afield with several different kinds of arrows in their quivers, each type suited to a different kind of game. Arrows with flu-flu fletching and blunt points are the safest combination when there is a possibility of hitting another person hidden by the cover.

Aside from flu-flus, most Indian arrows for war and hunting were fletched with three small lengths of feather, varying from about 1½ to 3½ inches. The quill was split, the fletching cut to the correct length, and the three vanes glued and lashed onto the shaft with slender thongs. A few tribes used no fletching at all; yet their hunters were successful.

Some tribes had a few expert bowyers and fletchers who spent most of their time making bows and arrows. It was these professionals who developed sinew-backed bows. These specialized, skilled artisans were highly regarded, and often the price paid for a good bow made by one of them was a horse. In most tribes, however, the hunter made his own gear.

The Indian bowman treated his tackle with great respect. He never kept his bow strung when it was not in use. Hunters often carried their thong bowstrings under their armpits to keep them dry in wet weather in order to avoid stretch. To prevent feathers becoming loose and matted, the Comanches and other mounted Indians often shot their precious arrows across a deep river before swimming across with their horses. The arrows were retrieved from the soft earth on the opposite bank.

MODERN BOWS AND ARROWS

The Indian bowman and the medieval European archer would be amazed if they could see and handle a modern target bow with all its accessories.

The typical modern target bow is usually a full working recurve, often five feet six inches long with a gleaming rosewood handle specially fitted to the grip of the user. The bow is made of chemically bonded layers of fiberglass and selected hardwoods. Protruding from the handle are two spring-loaded torque stabilizers that absorb shock when the arrow is loosed, sending it on a straight course. Fitted against the handle of the bow is a sliding aperture sight graduated in yards or meters.

The arrows for this bow are long aluminum tubes with steel target points, plastic nocks, and plastic vanes, which have largely replaced feathers in target shooting.

The cost of a fine target outfit is sometimes as much as $500, depending on quality and the amount of custom work that is done to fit it to the archer. With such tackle, a modern bowman is easily able to beat any archer using a hunting bow, but when it comes to stalking and taking game, complex target tackle is almost useless. Bowhunters use much less elaborate gear. Very few archers still use wooden bows. Laminated fiberglass and wood is favored for finely made bows, though a few cheap models are made entirely of solid fiberglass. These solid plastic bows are inferior to the laminated products, but they do have one great virtue—they are almost indestructible.

Choosing the Draw Weight

The draw weight of a bow is stated as the number of pounds of pull needed to bring it to a 28-inch draw. An experienced salesman in a good archery shop can give the purchaser much helpful advice on draw weight and other options, but the best way to find the right bow is to try out as many as you can until you find the correct length, fit, and "feel."

For first attempts at archery, a 40- or 50-pound longbow is usually adequate for a male adult. Later on, after muscles and skill develop, the beginner can graduate to a heavy hunting bow pulling 60 pounds or even more. A bow with a center arrow rest built into the handle is helpful.

Choosing the Bow Length

Bows between 45 and 66 inches in length perform well, though some archers prefer a longer bow because they find it shoots more

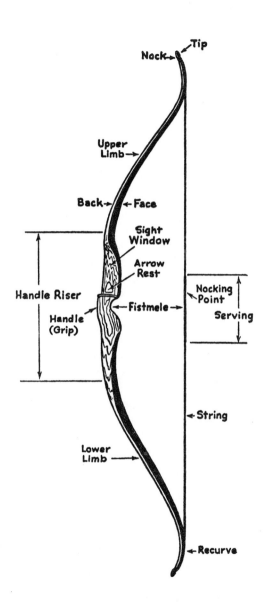

Modern Recurve Bow

smoothly. For archers who hunt in heavy cover, often from cramped blinds and stands, the manufacturers are now making extremely short, powerful, Indian-type bows, some only a little over three feet in length. These weapons resemble the bows used by many Woodland tribes for the same type of hunting. Because they are very sensitive to variations in grip and draw, they should only be used by those who really need and can handle them. Shooting one of these short bows affords some idea of the skill the Indian hunter must have had to use his crudely made, short wooden bow so effectively.

Choosing Arrows and Heads

Since the best bow cannot drive poor arrows straight, the hunting archer should buy the best arrows he can afford. The cost can be reduced by buying shafts, heads, and fletching separately, along with the necessary cements, and assembling the arrows in a home workshop. The homemade product can be modified to suit the individual archer's style just as the Indian hunter suited himself when making up his arrows.

Arrows with cedar shafts are still being manufactured, but aluminum and fiberglass are stronger and much more popular. Most bowhunters favor fiberglass because of its toughness and resilience.

Arrows with many different types of points and heads are manufactured, approximating the main types used by the Indians.

Target points are usually made with a hollow base that fits over the shaft. These points are round in cross-section and have no cutting edge. They are useless for deer hunting or any fairly large game because they do not cause much bleeding. Indian youngsters were started out with simple wooden shafts sharpened at one end for their target practice.

A bullet from a modern firearm kills by shock and much destruction of tissue. Arrows kill mostly by causing severe bleeding—unless the bowhunter cuts the spinal cord or puts the arrow directly into the heart. Therefore, archery manufacturers offer a wide variety of two-edged (single-bladed), three-edged, and even four- and six-edged heads. One head has two long edges in the form of partial spirals that cut a large figure-8 hole, but this head is difficult to sharpen. Heads for small game include blunts and those with light treble or even quadruple barbed points sometimes used for birds. Bowfishing arrows with harpoon points are also available. For blunts, many archers use empty .38 revolver cases, primer end forward, over the shafts.

Most modern archery tackle is durable and requires little care beyond thorough cleaning once in a while. A fiberglass-and-wood bow with a synthetic string can be kept strung all the time the hunter is afield, though it should be unbraced in camp and at home. Modern arrows and bows are almost impervious to water; the bows retain their flexibility and pull even when it is very damp or actually raining. Few Indian archers would try for game in the rain because their bows lost their pull. The Indian hunter was obliged to keep his bow unstrung until he saw his quarry or until tracks and other signs indicated that game was nearby.

INSTINCTIVE AIMING OF THE INDIANS

When an anthropological expedition came across a primitive Brazilian Indian tribe a few years ago, they came into contact with Indian hunters who had never used firearms. There was an excellent opportunity to study the natural, uncorrupted archery style of the primitive tribesman. A young member of the expedition who happened to be an enthusiastic bowhunter and target archer took careful note of the natural bowhunting techniques of these Indians.

They shot instinctively, without apparent aim. The bow was drawn and the arrow released as soon as the hunter got a clear shot. In one very difficult form of shooting, they could pick a jungle bird out of a 60-foot tree, shooting almost straight up. They also succeeded in arrowing large fish that showed themselves for only a second or two on the surface. In that type of shooting, there is no opportunity to take careful, considered aim. Their bows were strong and their cane arrows had good penetration on large game. The anthropologist saw them kill a big tapir, a heavy-muscled animal.

The observer found that the tribesmen shot well as long as the target was no farther than 50 yards away. When they tried to shoot at a greater range, accuracy and penetration fell off badly.

The white archer soon realized that these Indian hunters were not interested in long-range shooting. Because Indians hunted in the jungle where game cannot be seen at long range, and much of their hunting was done in such thick cover that most of their shots were taken at 60 feet rather than 60 yards, their archery tackle had been developed exclusively for short-range hunting, and it was admirably suited for that purpose.

Ishi, Indian Archer Extraordinary

In a different situation, another modern archer had the opportunity to study an untrained, natural Indian archer and his tackle. In 1911, a lone Indian was found near a slaughtering corral in California. His name was Ishi, and for many years, he had lived alone among the brushy-covered hills near Oroville. He was the last survivor of the Yana tribal group, and only superb skills in the woods had preserved his life when he lived in hiding from the encroaching whites who had killed or captured all his people.

Later, Ishi lived at the San Francisco branch of the University of California, where he made many bows, arrows, lances, and other hunting gear, and became a living exhibition. Dr. Saxton Pope, the well-known hunting archer, was one of the people who cared for Ishi, and he learned much from him.

Ishi's bows were a little over four feet long, made from mountain juniper. The draw weight was about forty pounds. The string was made from deer sinew that Ishi stripped between his teeth until it was long and thin. His arrows were tipped with obsidian or glass points. In the museum, he made points by flaking obsidian or glass with a wooden tool tipped with a piece of deer antler.

Ishi hunted deer with some of his white friends from the museum, and he described many of his previous hunts. From all this emerges the picture of a short-range hunter who shot from cover after approaching the deer very closely or lying in ambush for the animal. With a 40-pound bow, it was impossible to kill at long range, and Ishi, like most Indian hunters, did not need to shoot at long range. He was an expert at shooting from cramped positions while standing, kneeling, sitting, and crouching, and he had the patience to wait motionless for hours no matter how cold or hot it was, or how viciously the insects bit. This stoicism was one of the Indian's secrets of success in hunting.

Ishi could shoot instinctively without seeming to take aim at all though he sometimes did take careful, slow aim to make a difficult shot.

MODERN METHODS OF AIMING

Instinctive aiming differs markedly from the style followed by most modern bowhunters. The skilled American bowhunter knows the trajectory of his arrow from full draw. Pulling his bow so that his right hand comes back to its accustomed anchor—often the right cheekbone or side of the chin rather than the lips as in target archery—the bowhunter sights by holding the arrowhead above, on, or below the game he intends to hit, depending on his estimate of the range. The system is much like the "Kentucky elevation" used by many riflemen. If the game is close, the rifle's sights or the arrow's point must be held below the animal. At optimum range, they may be held dead on. At long range, they must be held over, the exact amount of holdover depending on the range. The key to this form of shooting is an accurate, quick estimate of the range.

In addition to solving the elevation problem, the archer, like the rifleman, must solve the windage problem. The consciously aiming archer must allow for the wind by holding left or right depending on how hard the wind blows and from what angle.

Bowsights

Complex mechanical and glass bowsights are popular in some forms of target archery in which the distance to the target is known in advance, and the sights can be set for that exact distance before the archer shoots. This type of shooting is of little use to bowhunters, who have to judge distance and shoot fast. Most hunters set rifle sights for an intermediate range and rely on Kentucky windage and elevation.

PRACTICE METHODS
FOR THE MODERN ARCHER

It is possible for the modern bowhunter to develop an instinctive aim, but acquiring this art is difficult and time-consuming. Unless the would-be instinctive archer has extraordinary coordination and senses, he must shoot thousands of shafts in practice before he achieves unthinking, unerring ability to make hits that would compare with the skill of a good Indian hunter. Only a few modern archers have achieved it.

The Indian youngster grew up with a bow in his hand and shot at targets and small game for years before attempting to down a deer, a bear, or any other big game. This continuous practice with successively more powerful bows and longer arrows developed the instinctive sighting that is the mark of a master bowhunter. Range estimation becomes automatic with enough practice, and though careful aim is achieved, it is done so swiftly and instinctively that the archer is not conscious of it.

Roving

For most of us, the amount of practice required makes it impossible to shoot like an Indian, particularly if one starts late in life. But if an archer wishes to try it, and has the necessary time, one way is to put in a lot of time at "roving." The archer simply walks through wooded country and shoots at various targets—the center of a clay bank, a tuft of grass, a soft stump, or anything that will not damage the arrows. For this type of practice, many bowhunters use special field points of the same grain weight as the hunting broadheads they intend to use later. Field points have a rather long, thin point, but it is round and does not have sharp cutting edges like a hunting broadhead. The essence of roving is to select the target quickly and shoot as fast as possible. It is excellent practice for developing an instinctive aim and also a deliberate one. This form of practice works well with a partner. By turns, one man selects the target for the other, trying to surprise the shooter by choosing odd targets at odd angles and varying distances.

Field-Archery Practice

The next-best method of bowhunting practice is to make use of a field-archery course. In target archery, the distance to the target is always known in advance, and the archer looses a series of shafts at each target over cleared, flat ground. In a field-archery course, a series of targets is placed at varying distances from the same number of shooting stations. The course is usually laid out along a winding path in wooded country. The archer shoots when he comes to a shooting station and sees a target.

These courses simulate average hunting conditions, especially when an archer forces himself to shoot quickly. After the archer memorizes each target, field archery begins to resemble more formal target archery, and many field-archery courses have been greatly modified to make the shooting easier so that more people would find it worthwhile to participate. On many courses, the distance to each target from the shooting point is posted on a small sign; so the archer does not need to make a range estimate, and uses the predetermined distance rather than his own judgment.

One solution to this problem is to have a friend move the targets for you before you shoot, but this usually can be done only on a very informal course where your fellow-archers are more interested in hunting than they are in high field-archery scores in tournament competition.

Whether your aim is deliberate or instinctive, the only way to perfect it is by constant practice.

Draw and Release

Developing a good method of holding the arrow on the string when drawing is very important. The Indians in the United States used a wide variety of holds, and the ancestry of some tribes has been traced in part by the particular method the tribal group used. Strangely enough, Ishi used a release that closely resembles one that was employed by tribesmen in Siberia. He hooked his thumb around the string and pushed the nock up against it with his other fingers! That kind of release proves very awkward to most modern archers.

In the United States, almost all target archers and bowhunters use the English release. This puts the index finger on top of the nocked arrow and the next two fingers below it. The little finger does not hook around the string like the other fingers, and the thumb does not touch the arrow at all.

A smooth draw and release help accuracy greatly. If you open your hand smoothly to release, thus avoiding a convulsive shock, you have a much better chance to shoot accurately. Shooting tabs or a shooting glove to protect the fingertips and a leather armguard on the bow wrist help a lot because they prevent injury and sore fingers. The archer is therefore less anxious to loose the drawn arrow in a hurry. Many Indians used decorative wide bracelets on their left wrists, but their hands were tough enough so that gloves and tabs were not required, and few Indians shot very powerful bows.

A carefully made string helps too. If the archer is confident in his string and does not fear that it will break and injure him, he's much more relaxed in his shooting; so his release will be smoother. Indian bowstrings were carefully made and frequently checked. As soon as a sinew or leather-thong bowstring showed signs of wear, it was discarded.

Modern bowstrings are usually made of some nonstretch synthetic fabric such as Dacron. A good bowhunter experiments until he finds the best nocking point on the bowstring. The string is then "served" with dental floss or silk. That is, the string is wrapped with some strong, smooth fiber to prevent fraying or wear where it contacts the arrow. Two or three inches of serving is enough. On top of this serving, the archer usually forms a nocking point by wrapping on an additional layer of serving fiber. Depending on the archer's shooting style, the nocking-point wrapping is placed either above or under the arrow. Some prefer a wrap above the nock and one below.

A predetermined nocking point of this kind has two advantages, and some Indian hunters used them. First of all, it gives the archer the advantage of uniform placement of his arrow on the string for every shot. In addition, the bowhunter finds that a well-placed nocking wrap allows him to place the arrow on the string without looking away from the game. If, for instance, one shaft is already buried in a deer but a second is needed to make the kill, it's very useful to keep your eyes on the animal or even walk toward it while fitting the second shaft to the string by touch alone.

Stance

The bowhunter must be able to shoot from cramped blinds, to left or right, and up or down a slope. Those who shoot from a perch or a platform (where legal) in a tree must be able to shoot almost straight down, often from a very cramped position. A hunting archer should be able to shoot from a deep crouch or when kneeling in order to keep head and shoulders low to the ground or below the tops of grass or brush. In other words, the modern bowhunter should be able to duplicate Ishi's shooting stances. Target archers try to develop a uniform, erect style for each shot they make because the object is repetitious precision at a known distance.

Fortunately, working on various shooting stances is possible indoors. Practice your draw sitting down, kneeling, inclining to one side, and in other cramped positions you may have to use when hunting. You can shoot with a good backstop even in the cellar, but just drawing the arrow and then easing it back is also good practice. That slow let-down after full draw is excellent for developing archery muscles too.

BOWFISHING

Stalking big fish with bow and arrow is an exciting way to fish. When hunting by boat, the silent, stealthy part of the hunt falls to the paddler or oarsman until he puts the archer within range of the quarry. The Indian archer shot the fish from the bow of the canoe or boat with a harpoon-tipped arrow with line attached, and sometimes the paddler had to help him to boat the catch since Indians took many very large fish, including cod, salmon, and sturgeon, this way. Today, the law prohibits taking freshwater game fish with spears or arrows, but the bowfisherman on fresh water still goes after rough fish such as carp and catfish. On salt water, almost any fish is legal game, but it is difficult to stalk fish on open salt water. There is too much room for the moving fish; therefore the bowfisherman usually takes the less-active species such as sharks and rays.

Some bowfishermen work in pairs as the Indians did when taking heavy fish. The archer arrows the fish, and the oarsman or paddler then seizes the line or the rod and reel. If the fish is large enough, the man with the line or rod has some sport too. Many modern bowfishermen use a single drum attached to the bow with the line wound around it. The line runs off the stationary drum much like the line coming off a spinning reel. Some bowfishermen tape a spinning reel to their bows.

Manufactured fletching, supplied with bowfishing arrows, is usually made of rubber or plastic, but many bowfishermen strip it off because the range at which shots are taken is so short that it is not necessary, and the removal of the fletching makes line tangles less frequent.

Retrieving Arrows

Many arrows can be lost while bowfishing; so it's best to use old, cheap ones. Wooden arrows often float to the surface if you miss when hunting small fish without a line attached to the shaft. If the shot is a hit, the arrow sometimes pins the fish to the bottom. Arrow and fish are recovered together, provided the water is shallow. If the water is too deep, an arrow stuck in the bottom is easily recovered with a noose weighted with a sinker. Drop the loop over the end of the arrow, and you will usually be able to close the noose over the shaft.

Many bowfishermen attached the line to the harpoon point rather than to the rear end of the shaft alone because wooden shafts often broke when a large fish was being played. One way to do this was to drill a small hole through the rear end of the wood shaft. The line was run through this hole, down the shaft, and then tied to the hole or ring in the harpoon head. Today, most bowfishermen use fiberglass shafts, which seldom break; so most archers attach their lines or leaders directly to the harpoon points.

Disengaging Harpoon Heads

Most harpoon heads have a single barb that is easily depressed and held in position by a spring catch. After a fish is brought in, drive the head all the way through the fish. Depress the point and withdraw the shaft. If the harpoon barb is of the fixed type, push the arrow all the way through the fish to remove it and then detach the line. Any attempt to pull a fixed barb back through a fish will tear up much of the edible portions.

Using Buoys as Drags

For big fish such as sharks, rays, and large catfish, the Indians often used inflated animal bladders or skins as buoys on the end of their lines. The fish was arrowed with a harpoon point, and the buoy thrown overboard. The fish tired itself by towing the buoy and working against it when sounding; so the fish was usually hauled in after a short wait. If not, a second arrow without line attachment was often used to kill the fish. Modern archers use a big piece of cork, a plastic container, or even an inflated inner tube as floats.

Trolling

When fishing from a seagoing boat, some bowmen troll lures without hooks, a rigged fish, or a chunk of meat (for sharks) behind the boat. When the trolled lure or bait brings a fish within range, the archer goes into action. A chum line of ground-up oily fish such as anchovies or menhaden also works well.

Deceptive Underwater Distances

In clear water, the archer frequently underestimates the depth, and the deflected arrow fails to penetrate deeply enough to enter the fish. Refraction of light from the water's surface can cause a fish to appear to be several inches from its actual location. Only practice allows the bowfisherman to overcome these two difficulties.

WINGSHOOTING

Little is known about wingshooting with bow and arrow by the American Indian, and some authorities believe that it was seldom practiced. The Indian was primarily after meat, and took most game birds with traps, nets, and snares. He did not have pointing dogs to aid him in wingshooting, which made that art very difficult. When the Indian shot birds, he probably preferred to shoot them on the ground or when they were perching or resting on the water. Today, going into thick cover after woodcock with bow and arrow presents problems which are hard to overcome, but that's the challenge of bowhunting. The difficulty enhances the sport.

There are many game birds in the United States. They include the various geese and ducks, grouse, chukar partridge, Hungarian partridge, pheasant, the band-tailed pigeon, two kinds of dove, ptarmigan, about eight kinds of quail, the wild turkey, the woodcock, the gallinules, the rails, snipe, the prairie chickens, and the little brown crane. Before there were any game laws (or any white men to make their enactment necessary), the Indian took many birds with archery gear that are now no longer legal game for anyone — curlews, herons, ibises, swans, and many more. Some of these birds are very large.

Of present-day game birds, the pheasant and the two partridges were introduced by the white man and, therefore, they could not have been hunted by the Indians. Of the remaining legal birds, only the goose, the wild turkey, the little brown crane, and the sage grouse cock are large enough to offer wingshooting targets for archers. Cock sage grouse weigh as much as six pounds, and the wild turkey and the Canada goose often weigh 20 pounds. By contrast, a bobwhite quail is about 10½ inches in length at most and weighs about 5½ ounces. To hit a quail on the wing with an arrow is usually done either by accident, or when shooting into a flock of these birds.

The tribal Indian hunter generally shot large birds on the ground if he could possibly do so and only attempted a wingshot with his bow if the bird was in flight and he had no other choice. It seems very unlikely that any tribal groups practiced wingshooting to harvest game, or as a contest. Modern Eskimos, for instance, use nets, snares, throwing sticks, and many other devices to take birds on the ground, on water, and on the ice. Even those who have shotguns prefer to shoot stationary birds and only fire at them on the wing when there is no other way. It is often easier to kill a water bird with a shotgun just as it rises from the water, and this was usually done by market hunters. In the water, a goose or duck is partially protected from the shot by the water. Just rising off the water, the bird is not yet flying fast enough to make a difficult target.

Some idea of the difficulty of taking game birds with archery tackle can be gained from studying the practices of modern archers. An informal study of bowhunting archers who went after pheasants concluded that one hit out of twelve is the best that a fairly skilled man can expect. Pheasants are large birds compared to quail, ptarmigan, doves, and many others. Today, bowhunters who take pheasants do so by shooting them on the ground ahead of a pointing dog most of the time, but if a bird does get up, a quick shot may score.

There is another revealing source of information on wingshooting with the bow. After the Civil War, two Confederate veterans, Maurice and Will Thompson, decided to leave civilization and all its cares and live like Indians. They experimented with wingshooting, using archery gear that they made themselves on Indian models, and the results were reported in Maurice Thompson's book, *The Witchery of Archery*. If any two men ever hunted like Indians, they did.

In their experiment, the brothers shot cane arrows at rails — slow-flying game birds of the marshes. The results are given as follows: Maurice shot 98 arrows at rails, lost 77 arrows, but killed 16 birds on the wing. His brother Will shot 121 arrows, lost 46, and killed 19 birds in flight. That's 219 arrows shot and 35 birds killed on the wing, or about six arrows for each bird downed. These birds were rails—much smaller and thinner than the pheasant, the modern wingshooting archer's usual target.

The wild turkey was almost exterminated in the United States by 1919. Afterward, wise conservation measures have gradually built up stocks of this magnificent game bird, and state after state has announced open season on them. The wild turkey is the only native bird that modern bowhunters try for regularly. It is also one of the world's largest birds, and most bowhunters shoot them on the ground. A few successful tries at wingshooting have been made, but most of them were last-minute decisions when the archer let fly at a bird that flew instead of running, which turkeys usually do. Archers who hunt the turkey do it in much the same way as the firearms hunter. They call the birds or stillhunt them. It's difficult enough to call up a legal bird or stalk one to reasonable range without taking on the still more difficult task of hitting them with arrows on the wing, though for adventurous bowhunters, it is an interesting experiment.

Today, few archers go after perching or sitting birds. Most of them prefer to hunt deer or call four-footed varmints. Very few men try wingshooting, and still fewer men manage to hit much when they do.

Practice in Aiming at Moving Targets

If you would like to try wingshooting with a bow, a little practice on moving targets will give some idea of its difficulty. Rig up a pulley arrangement and hang an ordinary balloon on it to represent the bird. Then stand off fifteen or twenty yards, and have a friend operate the line to pull the balloon along on a steady, horizontal course. Now try to hit the target. It's difficult even when you try from an acute angle, but if you try a straight crossing shot, it becomes much harder. As shotgunners learn after a while, a straight, going-away shot is easiest. Sometimes, the speeding bird seems to hang stationary in the air when it's a straightaway, but unfortunately, that's a rare shot. Most game birds are much more erratic. Woodcock seem to float straight up into the air when flushed and then veer and zigzag away at any angle in a steeply descending flight. Some bobwhites seem to be unable to fly in a straight line, and doves always seem to offer wide-angle crossing shots.

In all wingshooting, the instinctive aim is best. You have to shoot fast and lead the target, which makes slow, deliberate aim impossible.

When you can hit the balloon once in a while, put some sand in a small cloth bag and tie it closed. Have a friend toss it up for you. Instead of a straight flight as with the balloon on the pulley line, you'll get a curved flight. Try going-away shots first and then graduate to crossing shots.

When trying wingshooting in the field, remember that flu-flus are mandatory to limit the killing range of elevated shots so that you won't injure or kill someone in a neighboring field. Whenever possible, use blunt heads as further safety insurance, though it's hard to kill a large game bird such as a goose or a turkey with such an arrow.

MAKING YOUR OWN BOW AND ARROWS

If you train yourself to bowhunt like an Indian, why not make your own bow? This skill can be very useful in a survival situation.

Suppose that you have only a knife to start with. Go into the woods and select a good hardwood sapling of a kind that would make a good bow. Hack it down and start shaping your bow. Meanwhile, look for straight cedar or cane for shafts and try a quarry or broken ledge for suitable stone chips for arrowheads. From another successful hunter, you might beg the long sinews from a deer's hind legs for your first bowstring. Then snare a bird for feathers with which to fletch the arrows. Assemble the tackle, practice until you can shoot accurately, then go out and take a deer. A few modern archers have done this, and they really appreciate how skilled the Indian was.

After you have taken your first deer, no matter with what gear, a varied hunting career lies open before you. Modern archers have taken grizzly, polar, and brown bears; antelope; mountain goat and sheep; wolves; moose—and almost every species of North American big game. Farther afield, archers have taken tigers, elephant, and the ponderous African Cape buffalo with its armorlike, overlapping ribs. It is the boast of bowhunters that a skilled archer with the right tackle can take any game that a rifleman can kill, and the satisfaction of doing it lies partly in the fact that the archer is doing what the primitive bowhunter did. He proves himself equal to the native bowhunter in every part of the world.

4 /

Outguessing
The Wily Deer

IF YOU WANT to take a photograph of a prime whitetail buck, or want
to take one for venison and trophy with bow and arrow, shotgun,
handgun, or rifle, or you want to observe this magnificent game
animal in all his glory in wild surroundings—it takes Indian skills.

Unless you are content with a quick running shot with your weapon
or camera or only a glimpse of the animal, you must catch him
standing still or moving slowly at close range. To do so, you must understand the animal's habits and know something about hunting as
the Indians and the frontiersman hunted. Their lack of long-range
weapons and rifle scopes made close hunting a necessity, and very few
of them would chance a shot at a distant, running deer or other
animal. There was too much chance that the animal would get away,
and even a good flintlock rifle was a short-range weapon. If you can
hunt the whitetail in the way of the skilled Indian and frontier settler,
you'll be able to hunt almost any animal fairly well, and some of the
lessons learned will even come in handy with game birds.

The time to hunt the whitetail with camera is in the early fall. In
the winter, the whitetail is a poor specimen. The bucks shed their
antlers, and most of the animals are thin and unimpressive, with ribs
and backbones standing out as the beasts struggle to survive the cold

weather and scarcity of browse. All antlered animals are at their lowest ebb in February and March, when many starve unless hunting has thinned their numbers enough for the remaining animals to be carried over until spring by the available food.

In the spring, the whitetail greedily begins to fatten up on the opening buds, tender shoots, and ground plants. Does are followed by one or two fawns born late in the spring, and a male fawn may still be following the doe a year later, and a female fawn as much as two years later. Old, ragged winter coats are gradually shed and replaced by fresh, sleek hair.

In the spring, the buck's antlers sprout and begin to fork, since the male needs his weapons for the coming rut, when he often fights for the privilege of servicing a doe. Mature bucks live apart from the does and fawns most of the time, though you will sometimes see a spike buck still following his mother.

Late summer is a bad time for photographing and observing deer, and, of course, the hunting season is closed by law except in those states that permit a few weeks of early bow-and-arrow deer hunting. During that time people who live in the country will often see deer feeding in pastures, orchards, and fields. The animals seem to sense that no gunner is afield with blood in his eye. The bucks, however, are still in velvet, their antlers being covered with the soft, clothlike growth containing blood vessels that nourish the new horns. A photograph of a good buck still in velvet is an interesting addition to a collection of wildlife photographs, and it is not hard to get because even the large bucks often come out into the open to feed. Most photographers, however, want pictures of a prime buck showing the bare rack.

The rut comes at some time during the fall. In some states, the rut comes early, and in some others it is so late that it is going on even after the hunting season is over. The theory is that the time of the whitetail's breeding is determined by the coming of cold weather, but this is not always true. Sometimes the first nips of fall have not yet been felt, and yet the deer are already breeding. In other areas, at least part of the mating is going on during the firearms hunting season.

The early fall, before the opening of the firearms hunting season for deer, is the best time for the photographer or nature observer,

Whitetail Deer

especially if cold and winds have already stripped a large portion of the leaves from the trees. That is the time when some Woodland Indians tried to lay in a supply of deer meat that would last the entire winter.

During the rut, the bucks are less cautious than they usually are. In their desire to find a doe in heat, they sometimes become careless and blunder right into people and even enter farmyards. This is particularly true of forkhorns and other young deer. Even during the rut, however, the old, heavy-racked bucks show more caution. They did not attain their age and dignity by carelessly showing themselves, but it also may be true that the ancient bucks lose some of their interest in the does.

THE BOWHUNTER-PHOTOGRAPHER TEAM

The photographer and observer are usually afield when the bowhunter is going after deer. Almost everywhere, the game laws give the bow-and-arrow deer hunter three or four weeks to down his deer before the regular firearms hunting season (usually one or two weeks) opens. The bowhunter and the photographer make good companions afield. Both can be silent, and both are interested in close, standing shots.

It's unwise in most areas to go camera hunting during the firearms deer season, particularly if the law allows the use of high-powered rifles. If you do go afield then with a camera, be sure to wear bright hunting clothes so that you are easily identifiable as a man and not a deer. During the archery season, it is comparatively safe for bowhunters to wear camouflage clothing, but when firearms begin to go off, dress like a firearms hunter.

Often, a bowhunter and a photographer can team up, if the bowhunter uses a blind or a tree stand and he is experienced. The photographer can help in blind building and by making slow drives toward the hunter's stand. He may get a photograph or two during the drive. After the archer downs his deer, roles can be switched. Then the bowhunter, if he has the needed skills, can gently push deer to the photographer, who uses the bowhunter's blind or tree stand. Two good men working together can usually make quiet drives toward each other, and a team working together can set up a camp, build blinds, and do all the small chores easier than one man working alone.

TAKING ADVANTAGE OF
WIND AND AIR CURRENTS

Anyone who pursues deer has an ally and an enemy in the wind. Indian hunters often drove deer to strategically posted hunters in ambush. They moved with the wind if they could. The wind dispersed each driver's scent ahead of him and moved the deer out in front of the drivers so that the animals passed the standers at a slow enough pace to give the Indian archer an easy shot. This same method is often followed by modern firearms hunters. When hunting alone, the hunter or photographer, like his Indian predecessor, is careful to move against the wind. The moving air blows the hunter's scent to the rear, and he has a better chance of catching the deer standing.

What about situations in which there is little or no wind? Woodland Indians knew that it was wise to hunt at higher altitudes in the morning and lower ones in the evening. In the early morning—a good time to go after deer—the sun comes out and warms the air quickly. If you are on a high point, you will often see low ground fog in the valleys. Watch it, and you will see wisps of fog moving from low points toward crests. They dissipate before they move far, and the ground fog gradually burns off. The cold air in the low areas is warming, and it rises up the slopes. Of course, this does not happen if there is any appreciable wind. If there is enough wind, it quickly mixes the air, and there is no upward movement in the morning or corresponding downward movement in the evening.

As the sun goes down, the opposite process takes place. The air gradually cools, and there is a general downslope movement of the air. These upward and downward currents of air caused by temperature changes are so very gentle that a human being is seldom conscious of them, but this movement does carry human scent with it.

If you are hunting in the early morning, it's often best to walk quietly along ridges or take a stand on a high point. Your scent will be lifted high above you by the thermal current. In the evening, keep to the low areas between hills and ridges, but look upward toward the slopes and crests for a buck. The downward-moving air on a still day prevents your scent from rising. In some areas, though, the ground it-self shapes and focuses these air currents. You can't always depend on these air currents, but high hunting in the morning and keeping low in the late afternoon usually is best if there is no wind.

During mid-day, the air reaches a temperature balance on calm days and does not move up or down a slope. At such times, a careful hunter can move in any direction without danger of alarming an animal with his scent. In a calm, however, a human being's scent builds up and flows outward to a distance of about 20 or 30 feet if the hunter stands still. If you do try mid-day hunting then, and wish to move along, you can do so slowly but still keep ahead of your mount-ing scent. If you take a stand, you can be sure that your scent will not spread very far, but remember that a deer or other game animal may approach from any direction; there is no downwind and upwind.

FEEDING AND BEDDING HABITS OF DEER

As hunting pressure increases, deer gradually abandon normal day-time browsing and feed mostly at night. During a heavy firearms hunting season, it's almost impossible to catch sight of a deer during broad daylight. The deer are feeding at night and bedding down during the day. Mule deer out West, elk, and even moose often follow the same pattern if there are enough hunters afield. Antlered animals sense what is happening as soon as they hear the first few rifle or shotgun blasts. Bowhunters alarm the deer in a quieter way and do not force them to feed at night unless there is a heavy concentration of archers in one small area. This sometimes happened on tribal hunting grounds too, but the Indian could hunt at night with a jacklight or set snares for the deer.

If the deer are feeding at night and bedding down quietly in thick cover during the daytime, the best time to catch them with camera or weapon is during the early morning when the deer move from feeding ground to their daytime beds in thick cover or in the late afternoon when they are leaving their lie-ups to go to feeding areas.

It's always easier to catch sight of deer when the animal is on its feet. Bedding animals select quiet, concealed haunts in which to laze and drowse, and it is difficult to see the animals. The hunter must al-most step on the deer to discover them, and for such situations, the big drive employing many men often works best. Sometimes a line of drivers moving abreast can start deer up out of their beds, especially if a local man knows where the deer usually bed. Getting a shot is something else again. If you must shoot bucks only, it's often very hard to "see horns" when a deer jumps up and runs in very thick cover. In this situation, a few standers posted ahead of the drivers often have the best chance of getting a shot. After drivers have driven them out of their beds, deer usually run at high speed for only a short distance, slow down, and move with more caution.

Whitetails are local animals. They do not migrate, and they dislike long travel of any kind. The Indians knew this and prized a whitetail hunting ground. Provided the Indians did not kill too many deer at one time, one after another could be taken from a small patch of favored woodland. The whitetail can live close to man, and farming country often produces more deer than the deep woods. Whitetails do not like to be driven away from their familiar bedding and feeding areas, and if driven out, they soon return. Drivers often get shots at deer that try to circle back. Some wise old bucks, of course, know all about drivers and standers. When a hunter follows, they seem to realize that another man is apt to be waiting up ahead; therefore, the old bucks make a practice of sneaking back through a line of drivers or circling around a lone hunter.

To get behind a hunter, a tall buck often moves along cautiously, crouched low to the ground, with his rack laid back over his shoulders. The brush slides off the antlers with ease and little noise, and the apparent bulk of the animal is surprisingly small. Big deer sometimes know enough to lie down quietly in a clump of thick brush or under a fallen tree until the hunter or hunters have passed. This is why a knowing hunter forces himself through thick cover and always looks behind him from time to time as he moves along.

RECOGNIZING DEER RUBS AND PAWINGS

As cold weather comes on, the buck feels the urge for a doe, and he is full of energy and strength. His slender neck thickens, and he begins to practice for the fights that accompany the rut by hooking brush and fighting saplings with his antlers. The buck seems to know that he may need to fight another buck for a doe, and he tests his weapons on shrubs and saplings. The deer keeps at it until he has scraped the bark off a sapling or patch of low brush. If he still has any velvet left on his antlers, this sparring with vegetation scrapes it off, and in some areas, the bucks seem to scrape the velvet off deliberately. You can sometimes find shreds of it lying on the ground.

The buck also begins to advertise his presence to the does by pawing the ground until the leaves and grass are stripped away from a small, round patch. As a rule, bucks stay close to rubs where they have stripped bark. If you find pawings and rubbings close together near a patch of heavy cover with a deer trail leading from it to a feeding area such as a cornfield or a clump of fresh young saplings, that is the place to hunt when the season opens or to set up with a camera before the bullets begin to fly.

DEER-HUNTING METHODS

Hunting with Dogs

The gentleman hunters of Europe rode to hounds when they hunted antlered game, bear or boar. Quite late in European history, they carried no firearms but this form of hunting was a noisy one. Hounds make a great deal of noise when they are pursuing four-footed game, and so do horsemen. The man who hunts alone on foot by tracking and stalking makes as little noise as he can. He is therefore called a stillhunter, and his method is called stillhunting, though the hunter does move about.

The American Indian sometimes used dogs for big game, including deer, elk, and bear, but that method was more often employed in the open country of the West than it was in the eastern woodlands. The big, nondescript dogs of the western Indians were used as burden carriers or pullers before the tribesmen acquired horses. The dogs were not bred to hunt and never developed the specialized nose of pureblooded hunting hounds. Some Indian tribes did use dogs and knew how to make a drive with them.

Only a few states, most of them in the South, allow hunters to use dogs for deer and bear. In the South, deer cover is so thick that a man would not get his deer without the help of a good pack. In these areas, the hunters use shotguns loaded with a charge of buckshot and take their stands much as the Indians did with bows and arrows. In fact, bow-and-arrow and a buckshot-loaded shotgun have about the same killing range. Most often, the success of a southern deer hunt depends on one or two local men who know the habits of the deer and understand their dogs. The leaders of the hunt decide where the standers are to be placed. Standers are usually posted in a line along a ridge, one side of a creek, a woods road, or parallel to some other obstacle the deer must cross. Care is taken to post a stander at every promising crossing. For instance, if the deer are to be driven across a narrow field, they will cross it by the shortest possible route from cover to cover. The same applies to streams and roads. Knowing the deer crossings helps standers to get shots. And yet, big old bucks seem to avoid established deer crossings; so it's wise for the stander to watch on all sides provided he does not move his head from side to side, making himself obvious to the deer.

The dog handlers take the pack around to the other side of the cover and release it. A good pack moves slowly, covering each yard of ground carefully for deer scent, but when a buck gets up or hot scent is struck, the dogs line out on the track and begin that spine-chilling baying that tells the standers that a deer may be headed their way. Quite commonly, the stander can only see 25 or 30 yards in thick cover and has just a fleeting chance for a shot, taken at a moving animal unless a buck tries to sneak through well ahead of the dogs. The stander can hear the dogs a long way off. By the time the buck comes through, many first-timers are so nervous that they can hardly handle their shotguns. The Indian hunter on stand with a baying pack driving a 1,000-pound bull elk in his direction had to have nerves that few white men possess. Elk and moose hunting with dogs is now prohibited by law.

Deploying Standers and Drivers

In the North, hunting deer with dogs is forbidden except in certain very brushy sections of Canada. Dogs are not necessary in most of the North because the cover is not so dense. In thick patches, men substitute for dogs. A line of standers is posted, and another group circles the patch of cover and drives toward the standers. In pine barrens and other thick cover, it is the custom to make a noisy drive. The drivers bark like dogs, howl, and yell as loud as they can. Indians sometimes used rattles and horns.

In more open country, quiet drives are more effective. The drivers move slowly and make as little noise as possible. Often, they stagger the line. One man at a time moves forward from the main line of drivers, hoping that he will get a buck up and that the deer will try to circle back through the line so that another driver will get a shot. Then another man in the line moves forward while the first driver stands still. The next driver to move may put a buck up that will move forward past the standing driver. Each man may be told to move forward in turn at 10- or 15-minute intervals. Standers may be posted ahead, but staggered drives can be effective.

A beginner is inclined to look for deer straight ahead when he is driving. He always seems to feel that he will get a going-away shot if any. Actually, the drivers often do get shots to one side or the other as the deer try to circle back.

The Indians often posted standers on the far side of a deep creek or small river. The drivers drove the animals into the water where archers could kill them as they swam. Often the drive was set up to trap the deer in the water between the standers and the drivers, and sometimes, canoes were used so that the deer could be killed from them. Many bucks and does were killed with the sharp edge of a canoe paddle swung against the base of the animal's skull. Lances and harpoons were used also.

Today, the law forbids killing most game while it is swimming, but there is no law against killing deer after they have left the water, and even a shallow stream provides an opening in the forest that deer must cross. Hunters also make expert use of other natural obstacles just as the Indians did before them.

A long ridge is a fine place to post standers, especially if the crest of the ridge is bald or thinly wooded. The standers take their posts just below the crest on the side away from the drivers to avoid showing themselves on the skyline. Sometimes the stander finds cover right on the crest, but it's enough as a rule to keep low with only the motionless head showing.

Most often, the deer try to stay on low ground. They try to get through notches in the ridge, but sometimes, you'll see a big buck making it hell for leather toward the highest crest out in the open when he could have followed a low notch. It's much more likely that spikes, forkhorns, and does will follow low ground, run established deer trails, and use well-worn crossings.

When a large group is driving with standers posted, it's important to handle your gun with care. This is one reason why southerners prefer a buckshot-loaded shotgun for deer driving. The killing range of the weapon is short; so it's almost impossible to kill another stander or a driver. To shoot a dog on a southern deer drive is tantamount to deliberate murder.

In most places, it is a cardinal hunting sin to leave your stand during a drive. If you do, the crossing is left uncovered, and you may also wander into the line of fire of another stander or an approaching driver. When rifles are used, and men are driving the deer, gun safety is of major importance. Other standers are within killing range of your weapon, and every stander knows that a driver will soon come out. Of course, no one should fire unless he is certain that the target is a legal deer. Drivers should know exactly where the standers are posted so that they can yell or blow a whistle before coming out to a stand. The danger is not as great as it may appear because the ground rolls a little. Deer hunting seldom takes place on flat ground—that's cropland in most places. If you make it a point to always have rising ground behind the deer when you shoot, the bullet will not carry very far. For this reason, conscientious hunters refuse to shoot at any game that appears on the skyline.

Combining Standing and Stillhunting

If a large group of men is not available or if a few hunters dislike big drives, a combination of stillhunting and standing is often best. Working alternately, one man hunts toward the other. Driving the deer to the stander is difficult in such a case because the animal can easily circle back behind the single driver.

The driver stillhunts. He moves quietly and slowly, almost as though he were hunting alone. One good way is to take 20 or 30 paces or even less and then stand stock still for a few minutes. Deer, in common with much other game, can often sense the hunter a long way off. Often, the buck will remain still to see if the hunter will pass by. If the hunter stands still for a few minutes, the animal or bird becomes increasingly nervous, until finally terror gets it up out of its bed or hide. The game seems to believe that it has been spotted because the hunter has stopped, and the strain becomes too much for the animal or bird and it breaks cover. Deer, black bear, elk, grouse, and many other animals and birds often follow the same pattern.

Standing and driving in pairs works well if both hunters know the country or are skilled enough to plan the hunt well when they first see the terrain. A topographical map helps, but studying the country before the season is best of all. Standing and driving in pairs is the only form of driving that usually works well for archers. A deer put up by a skilled *slow* stillhunter working toward a stander moves out at a leisurely pace, and the stander or even the driver may get a shot. A big, noisy drive moves the deer too fast for an archer. He cannot get on target in time to shoot. If only two men are standing and driving, the driver can cover much more territory if he zigzags.

Solo Stillhunting

The lone stillhunter takes to the woods hoping to bag game without the aid of drivers or dogs. The solo stillhunter has the greatest need for sharp senses and skill in the woods. On big, noisy drives, even a novice may get a buck if he is posted on a good stand.

As more and more men take to deer hunting, the tendency is for them to gang up for big drives, and the solo stillhunter is squeezed out of much territory by clubs that lease the land and acquire exclusive hunting privileges for their members. And yet, the lone stillhunter can cover numerous small pockets that deer clubs wouldn't bother to hunt.

In group hunting, scant attention is paid to the wind. Many group hunters never even check on wind direction. The objective is to drive deer to the standers, and it's better to hunt with the wind than against it. A stillhunter must check on the wind constantly, as the Indian did, since there is no stander waiting.

THE STORIES THAT TRACKS TELL

In big drives, tracks are often ignored except in preseason scouting. In a group drive, you can't deviate from your line of advance if you happen on a set of tracks that point to one side. You must complete the drive on schedule, and you must cover your lane toward the standers. A stander who comes off his stand to follow tracks, leaving a crossing uncovered, may wander into another man's line of fire.

Some solo stillhunters pay far too much attention to tracks, however. When the season is open and deer are being moved about by many hunters, you'll find tracks almost everywhere on a likely piece of ground. Two or three deer in a limited area will wander and give the hunter the impression that there are dozens of deer. You may also follow a set of tracks to the guts of a deer already shot and dragged out by another hunter.

Telling Doe from Buck Tracks

There is really no sure way to tell the difference between the tracks of a big doe and a buck, but there are a few guides that sometimes work. Big prints moving alone are often those of a mature buck. Yearling deer follow their dams, and one doe may even have a pair of twins following her. Since does and anterless fawns are usually protected by law, it is usually unwise to follow the tracks of a group of deer. Bucks move alone, but if the rut is still on, they may follow a doe. If you find tracks of does and fawns and then a big track joins them, there's a chance that you will soon come upon a buck.

Bucks seem to drag their feet a little more than does, and they therefore often make scrapes or drag marks behind each print in soft ground or snow when they are walking slowly, but this is not always so.

Figuring Out Which Tracks Are Fresh

It's sometimes difficult to tell the age of a given set of prints. On damp ground shaded by trees or brush, a week-old track may look very fresh. The disturbed pine needles or leaves may still be damp on their undersides, and the little clods of earth thrown up by a running

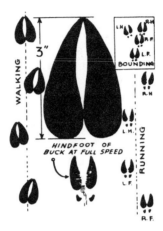

Whitetail Deer Tracks

deer may still be dark with moisture. Follow such a track long enough, and you'll probably come to a dry place. If the tracks there are still fresh, you are probably close to a deer.

Only good tracking snow makes the story clear, but it seldom seems to fall during the short deer-hunting season. Good tracking snow is slightly damp and takes prints well, and it falls the preceding night. If snow falls before you go hunting, every track is fresh. If snow is still falling when you begin to hunt, it may fill up the prints before you get close to the deer.

Identifying Tracks of Different Species

Novices often make very embarrassing mistakes in identifying tracks. A beginner once was very surprised when he found that a line of deer tracks led through a hole in a woven wire fence into the pigyard of a farm. He wondered how the deer had gotten through the small hole and what the animal wanted among the pigs. He didn't know that he had been following a big porker that had escaped from the swilling yard and was obviously returning in the evening to get his share of the swill. It sounds almost bizarre, and yet there are many "hunters" who cannot tell a deer's prints from those of swine, young beef cattle, and sheep. All have somewhat similar hoofs, and the tracks look alike to the inexperienced eye. In the South, where there are many wild razorback hogs wandering the woods, this type of mistake is easy to make. One way to avoid it is to pay attention to all kinds of animal tracks—domestic as well as wild—when you are visiting farming country. Can you, for instance, tell the track of a big domestic dog from those of the coyote, fox, and wolf? Few modern hunters can, but it can be very important. That is one of the first things young Indian hunters learned.

How Indians Followed a Set of Tracks for Days

Indian hunters and frontiersmen sometimes ran animals down by following the tracks of a single animal. When the hunter found a big deer, elk, or moose track, he followed that track until he got a shot or was forced to give up. If the hunt took several days, the hunter bivouacked out on the track at night. The hunter had a good chance to take a lot of meat if he caught up with his quarry.

When a hunter strikes a fresh track in new snow, it's sometimes worthwhile to follow it. After he jumps the animal once or twice, the animal becomes so frightened that its efforts to escape grow more feeble every time the hunter approaches, though sometimes a moose or a big bear will turn on the stillhunter who pushes too hard. Even wolves and coyotes can be hunted in this way on snow where they flounder and the tracker glides along on skis or snowshoes. Finally, the animal seems to give up hope, and his last attempt to escape from the hunter is so slow that a shot becomes possible.

This type of hunting used to be much more common than it is now. Indians knew how to do it, and they could move with speed and silence. Nowadays, the annual open season crops the game so evenly in most areas that any exceptional animal worth tracking for days is rare; so most hunters go after any legal deer, elk, or moose, and many eastern bear hunters do the same. Trophy hunters are much more likely to follow big tracks for long distances. In crowded areas, too, the tracker may push his quarry into the sights of another hunter. And there are "No Trespassing" and "Posted" signs to contend with. Though game animals can't read signs, they seem to sense that there are certain tracts where there is little or no hunting.

Studying Terrain While Following Tracks

The best use the solo stillhunter commonly makes of tracks nowadays is to locate game hangouts during the preseason scouting. If you do follow tracks on a hunt, don't keep your head bent to study the tracks while moving along. Indian trackers knew that the eyes should move constantly forward. You'll seldom track the animal right to its bed or hide. The deer, elk, or moose will often sense you coming and get up to move on, or if the animal is already on its feet, it will speed up as soon as it senses you. Be ready to click the shutter or shoot. If you keep looking at the tracks, you won't be ready, and may not even see the game. Remember too that antlered game, bears, coyotes, and wolves may circle back to see what is on their track and that foxes are experts at it. Keep an eye out to the side too, if possible, and look back over your shoulder. The hunter's dual problem is to see the tracks and follow them while studying new terrain in all directions. Impossible? Well, maybe it is, but a few men can do it, and most Indian hunters did it naturally.

The stillhunter makes use of the terrain. He moves forward, pausing often, until he comes to a high point from which he can see the next stretch of country. There he pauses to study thickets, draws, low spots, windfalls, and clumps of brush for game. If he's in open country out West after mule deer or antelope, he uses binoculars or a spotting scope to cover a great deal of territory. He can also use his rifle scope to study likely spots before moving on. Even in the East, in thick whitetail or moose country, binoculars or scope can be very useful. Glass the territory or the wall of trees or brush in front of you slowly—likely spots first, less likely spots last. Only after you are sure that you cannot catch a standing animal unawares should you leave your vantage point and move forward. Check right then on the wind. Has it shifted behind you? If so, you'll have to change direction unless there is a stander out in front of you.

PICKING THE DEER OUT
FROM ITS BACKGROUND

A novice just looks for a deer, elk, moose, or bear. He expects to see the entire animal, out in the open and standing still. A good hunter, like the Indian, looks for something that appears out of place where he is hunting. Having spotted something unusual, he studies it. Often it will grow and take shape. It increases in size and form until it becomes a buck deer staring straight at him, or a moose, head held low under the evergreens to study those strange objects that may be the hunter's knees and boots.

Look for parts of the game. For instance, dead black is very rare in nature. If you have seen bear tracks, be on the lookout for a patch of midnight black in the brush. If you locate it, don't move forward until you have studied it carefully. It may be a black bear's fur, partially hidden by leaves.

In mature woods, most of the objects close to the ground are vertical—tree trunks and saplings. In that kind of cover, look for horizontal lines. These horizontal objects are often easy to pick out. The light filters through the leaves overhead, and an animal's horizontal back seems to catch much more of the light than the vertical tree trunks. That faint horizontal luminosity in the dark woods is often the tipoff that results in meat in the pot, a rack on the wall, or a good photograph.

Don't shoot prematurely. Wait until that first sign or patch of odd light grows into the animal itself. If only part of the animal is visible, you cannot place a shot well.

THE CONTEST OF THE SENSES—
DEER'S AND MAN'S

The game is alert too and using all its senses to detect danger. Many experienced hunters will tell you that the whitetail deer has the best ears and sense of smell of any North American game animal, but the apparent superiority of the animal's senses may be due in part to its great intelligence. If you understand how the game you seek uses its senses to detect danger, you'll have a much better chance to score.

What Deer Can Scent

The whitetail's sense of smell is phenomenal, and the animal can scent a dog or a man when the wind and moisture are right at over 100 yards, and sometimes much more. On an average day, deer can be approached only from downwind. If you can remain silent, you sometimes get quite close.

How Deer Interpret What They Hear

The enormous ears of the western mule deer indicate acute hearing, and other deer are not far behind him. Yet, the animal must interpret what he hears. Deer seem to realize that a hunter usually moves rather slowly, and many Indians and some white men knew that a change of pace sometimes gets the big old bucks. Try charging into cover once in a while. Make enough noise to simulate a careless four-footed animal crashing through the brush, and a big buck may take you for a doe or some other large animal. This change of pace works on rare occasions even with big old deer. There are times when it is the hunter's only choice. If you know that a big buck is lying up in thick cover and the leaves and brush are very dry and noisy, you can't get to him by stealth, and the change of tactics may work.

Are Deer Color-blind?

There's much argument about the eyesight of deer. Some say that all deer are color-blind. Others believe that deer do see color and can interpret it. Hunters who wear bright clothing as protection against the carelessness of others do kill many antlered animals, some at close range; so it seems that deer are not as color-sensitive as human beings, waterfowl, and crows. On the other hand, most bowhunters wear camouflage. Since they must get much closer to the game than the rifleman, the blotchy camouflage cloth may break up the hunter's outline even though the deer may see only in shades of black and white.

Antlered animals do seem to detect shine. A bowhunter's bare face shining in a well-constructed evergreen blind is often enough to alarm a big buck. A camouflage face net helps. Soft-finish cloth for hunting clothes is preferable, since it does not scrape much on the brush when you move. Dyed, soft wool is very good. Select soft cloth that does not reflect much light even if it is brightly colored.

The Far-sighted Whitetail

Whitetails seem to be far-sighted. Some hunters say that the deer can spot a man moving at a considerable distance but that when the man is close, say under fifty yards, the deer's vision is less keen. Once inside the critical point, a hunter or photographer can come close if he moves in a slow and stealthy manner. If correct, this information is useful to photographers, bowhunters, shotgunners, those who hunt with handguns, and hunters who use muzzleloading, black powder shoulder arms. If you hunt with a modern high-powered rifle, 200 yards or even 300 is close enough.

The Deer's Limited Peripheral Vision

Antlered North American animals have eyes directed toward the front. Whitetails cannot see to the side very clearly, and cannot catch even a vague object slightly toward the rear. Indian hunters took advantage of this when stalking deer and elk. If they could spot a lone deer feeding on ground cover, they could often get within only ten or twelve yards—sure range for a bow or even a thrown lance. Of course, they approached from downwind. In addition, they moved only when the animal had its head down to feed. In that position, the animal cannot see the hunter even though he approaches from in front. When deer are feeding, especially whitetails, they often stop, raise their heads, and look all around. They may swing right around in a circle, tossing their heads, and then go back to feeding. A cautious hunter, walking upright, can walk right up to the animal, if the wind is right and he makes no noise, by moving only when the deer's head is down. When the deer begins to raise its head, the hunter stands motionless. Of course, this method should be used with only a single deer, or at the most, two. Feeding deer seem to take turns as lookouts. If there are more than two deer, there is scarcely a second when one of the animals is not looking around.

Weather That Dulls Deer's Senses

The deer's senses, even the whitetail's, seem to desert them on still, misty days, especially when there is sudden warm weather after cold. During cold, clear weather, deer are alert and spirited. The animal's senses are keyed up and tell him of any strange and possibly dangerous smell, sight, or sound even when distant. During damp, still, warm weather, the deer is less alert, and if conditions are favorable, he may not sense you until you are very close. Somehow, the mist seems to blunt the deer's eyesight more than it does a man's, and the warm, heavy air deadens hearing as well as sight. On such days, the hunter is actually superior to the deer because his sight functions well, while the deer's does not.

The Secret of Silent Stalking

Pay close attention to your feet. Try to avoid committing your weight to each step before you know that it will make little or no noise. The Indian gait is described often as "pigeon-toed," but that description is inaccurate. Most Indians pointed their toes straight ahead and walked tirelessly on the balls of their feet. Most white men put the weight on the heel; then the ball slaps down too. If you listen to most men walking on a hard surface, you'll discover that each step produces two noises, made by the heel and ball of the foot. There is no way to lessen the weight if an obstacle is encountered because the man strides along heavily and carelessly. If the heel doesn't snap a twig, the forward part of the foot will. Most white men also turn their toes outward to some extent so that the inner side of the foot is likely to catch obstacles. The Indian's walk is ideal for getting through thick growth quietly.

It is not necessary, however, to walk exactly like an Indian. If you try to point the feet straight forward when you are unaccustomed to it, the calves of your legs and ankles will soon give out under the strain. Yet, if you do pay attention to how you walk and try to do so quietly, you'll soon be walking more like an Indian or moccasin-wearing frontiersman with every mile covered. Try to feel with your toes so that you can withdraw your foot if you feel a noise-making obstruction underneath it. Without this ability, you'll have to look down much of the time to pick out suitable ground, and that will keep your eyes off the game. Some hunters seem to have 20/20 vision in each sole.

Learning to Distinguish Game Sounds

On big drives, hearing is unimportant. The drivers may deliberately make a great deal of noise, and there's little chance to hear game before you see it. The lone stillhunter has to hear well, or he misses many chances to see game. Hearing is important to the hunter of big, four-footed game such as whitetails and mule deer, but even the small-game hunter has great need of his ears.

Good hearing is important, but being able to interpret what you hear is even more important. The drumming of a ruffed grouse may sound to an inexperienced hunter like a pulp cutter some distance away starting a balky chain saw. The same thing applies to the noises made by big game. Can you identify the plaintive bleat of a fawn? If you can, it may lead you to the doe the fawn is following, and if you find the doe, the buck may not be far away.

No one can educate the ears of a stillhunter except himself, and aside from recordings of game sounds, there is only one way to do it. Go out into game country, take cover under some brush or build a blind, then listen. Don't sneeze, cough, smoke, or scratch that insect bite. Just sit there as long as you can remain silent. There are men who go hunting every year who have never done this, and in spite of twenty years or more of hunting, they are almost deaf in the woods. Since they are always on the move, they never learn to recognize the noises made by game—something that an Indian youngster learned long before he was allowed to hunt.

On reaching the patch of woods or other cover, you may see only a fleeting brown thrasher moving quickly away close to the ground or a grouse suddenly bursting out of cover and making for a distant ridge. After you remain still for half an hour, you should be accepted by most animals and birds nearby as a harmless part of the landscape even if you are not entirely hidden. A shrew may appear from the leaves at your feet, a downy woodpecker begin to drill only a few yards away, then a fox squirrel scramble in an oak only a few feet away; and perhaps you'll hear the strange sounds that turkeys make to gather the scattered flock. If you're lucky, you may even hear the soft shuffling of a buck in the leaves on the hardwood ridge and then see him moving cautiously down the deer trail toward food or shelter.

Hunters who have never tried listening before will be amazed at the scrapings, mutterings, calls, and mysterious noises that reign in the "silent" woods.

TRAIL-WATCHING

The trail-watcher who goes after deer has great need of keen senses. Preseason scouting helps him to locate a likely stand upwind from a crossing where he has seen recent pawings or buck rubs. He may take his stand in natural cover or he may build a blind. The lone trail-watcher hopes that a legal deer or other big game will come by, usually early in the morning or late in the afternoon. During mid-day, some trail-watchers come off their stands and stillhunt for a while.

A good trail-watcher makes an excellent stander on a deer drive because he knows how to wait quietly and take advantage of everything he sees or hears, but most skilled trail-watchers hunt alone. They know their territory and the game, and drivers would not be of much help. Some trail-watchers do take advantage of other deer hunters by posting themselves on runways where they know deer may pass because they are fleeing from big drives nearby.

Trail-watching in really wild country requires great patience unless the trail-watcher has successfully used the blind or stand before. You have to select the right spot for a stand, and that takes a great deal of skill. The country is so big that the wilderness trail-watcher knows the deer may be almost anywhere within an area of many square miles. If preseason scouting has shown a lot of sign, the deer will probably be nearby.

Closer to civilization, trail-watching may be even harder. After the hunter is on stand, he needs mental discipline to stay on it. Now and then a rifle or shotgun goes off in the distance, and the trail-watcher begins to imagine that the deer are crowded together over in the next valley where stillhunters, standers, and drivers are knocking them down in droves. Yet, many men shoot wildly, and a dozen shots may mean only that one forkhorn has been tagged. If you have selected your stand with care, have faith in it, and it will often pay off.

The Indian hunter knew his hunting ground well and often followed a trail-watching method that is neglected by most modern bowhunters and gunners. Because he knew the ground, he could pick out several good crossings. If others reported deer in one particular part of his territory, the Indian hunter usually knew a likely stand in that area. If the wind blew in an unfavorable direction for a particular stand, he could move quickly to another where the crossing was upwind. Few modern hunters bother to select several good trail-watching stands. Even fewer build several blinds, each one in a promising location, though it's one of the best ways to fill your license.

Calling Deer

If the rut is still on, trail-watchers and some standers sometimes call deer by rubbing and rattling two old antlers together to imitate a fight between bucks. Often, a buck will rush up to get in on the battle, perhaps hoping that there is a ready doe nearby. In some states, this form of calling is forbidden by law because it is too effective when the bucks are in a rutting frenzy.

Most people who rattle for the first time make too much noise. After the first rush and shock, deer usually back off and wait for some time, apparently to get up courage again. As combat continues, the deer tire and the rattling comes at longer and longer intervals. If you rattle antlers too much, it sounds unnatural. Instead of using old antlers picked up after they have been dropped by the deer or cut from last year's kill, some hunters use hardwood sticks because they are easier to carry. Hardwood rattling is more difficult than using the real thing. Wood doesn't produce the right tone unless the caller knows how to handle the sticks.

Some hunters imitate the bleat of a fawn with their mouths or an artificial call, and this is especially effective if does may be taken. Many does will respond to the bleating of a lost fawn even though they do not have fawns of their own. Even bucks will sometimes come to a well-imitated fawn bleat, as the Indians knew. Perhaps they do so in hopes that the dam is nearby.

Attempting to call deer with the fawn bleat is risky. The deer season in most states is short, and you may frighten off the only chance for a shot if your imitation is not perfect.

Whitetails also make one other sound—the whistling snort of the buck when he is puzzled, alarmed, or angry. The hunter or photographer often hears it when he cannot see the deer but the deer has sensed the man. At those times, it pays off to remain absolutely still and give the deer the next move. The buck knows that a man is somewhere nearby, but cannot pinpoint him. The animal is trying to decide in which direction to run. If the man waits, the deer may come toward him. If he tries to call the deer or move toward him, he reveals his location, and that's when a big buck vanishes.

5 /

Reading Tracks and Foreseeing Animal Moves

AFTER A BOY or a man has taken a fair share of squirrels and rabbits and has scored on a few deer as a lone stillhunter, he begins to develop something akin to the skill of an Indian hunter or frontiersman. He starts doing the right thing at the right time without thinking about it much. That type of skill can't be learned from any book, but there are some useful things that a book can point out.

The tracks in this book appear on the page as they would in soft snow, damp sand, or mud, though clear prints are rare on the leaf-strewn forest floor or on hard, dry ground. The experienced tracker going into a new region seeks out likely areas where he can find clear prints in order to take his own census of the animals in the area. Good trappers are expert at it, and Indian hunters were good too. The trapper doesn't think in terms of exact numbers, but somehow, the tracks that he finds tell him whether or not there are enough pelts in the area to make running a trapline there worthwhile.

TIPS ON HARD-TO-FOLLOW TRACKS

Tracks are often distorted, and you may see only disturbed leaves, clots of thrown-up earth, bent grass, broken twigs, and other clues running in a line. You often can't tell what animal made them unless you follow them for a while. The animal will probably cross a soft spot, and then you may find just one clear print of one foot.

The Problem of Dead-End Tracks

After identifying the tracks and deciding to follow them, don't step right on the tracks. Sometimes a fox or coyote will suddenly reverse himself and step in his own tracks to get back to a piece of cover where he can jump aside. That leaves a baffling dead end for the tracker, especially if he has obliterated the animal's tracks by walking on them so that he can't backtrack and find the jumping-off place. Sometimes, the track cannot be followed to the animal, but backtracking may lead to the animal's den or lie-up and a shot or a photograph. If the hunter or the photographer suddenly comes to a dead end in the tracks, the animal has backtracked in its own prints (or close to them), or it has jumped to a leaning tree, log, stone wall, or other object well off the ground. Coons and foxes are experts at this. Do as the Indian hunters did. Look around at the dead end for such a means of escape, and if you don't find one, try backtracking. Sometimes you'll see one or two prints that missed the original ones, and they may point in the opposite direction.

Some animals are very clever about entering water to throw a tracker off. If the tracks you're following enter a stream and do not come out again on the opposite side, the animal has probably walked along in the water for a while to throw the pursuer off. Many animals are quick to sense when a predator or a hunter is on their trail. Foxes, bears, and some other animals often circle back to identify their pursuer or get the scent.

Changing the Angle of Vision

The light is very important because of the shadows it throws. From one angle, the tracks may be almost invisible unless you look closely. From another angle with favorable light, the line of slight depressions or disturbed earth or leaves is clear because of the shadows that they cast. If tracks fade or disappear, try the Indian trick of moving from side to side to get the light right.

Interpreting an Animal's Line of Advance

In order to keep your eyes off the ground so that you can spot the animal ahead, it helps if you can deduce the line of advance and move from point to point. Deer, for instance, especially those with large antlers, will almost always take the easiest way unless pushed hard and trying to conceal themselves. They find it difficult to force their racks through thick cover. An otter on dry land will almost always be moving toward the nearest water. Foxes usually move from thick cover to thick cover, but sometimes pause on high ground to sun themselves and look around. During late fall, most bears are making beelines to nut groves, bee trees, berry patches, and other sources of food in their haste to fatten up before hibernation.

Move fairly fast from point to point, checking now and then to make sure that the line of prints is still there. Some Indian trackers were so good at this that they seldom looked at the tracks. They almost read the animal's mind, knowing what it was looking for or traveling toward, and they could follow the route more by knowing what the animal wanted than by doggedly following the prints that it had made.

If you lose the tracks, circling ahead will often cut them again. Go back to the last prints, pause a while, and try to figure out the route. See if you can locate any terrain feature that would have caused a sudden change of direction. If so, it may be profitable to make a circle in that direction. Remember, though, that it is difficult to pick up a line of faint tracks or sign when you cut it from the side. The tracks are under your eyes only for a few seconds as you move along, and you may have to make several circles.

WHEN TO FREEZE

A good trail-watcher stays as quiet as possible while waiting for game, but sooner or later has to move camera or weapon to take a shot. Stillhunters and trackers must move along even if they do so slowly. At the first sight of the game, is it best to make an instant shot or freeze in your tracks and raise your weapon or camera in a deliberate manner? There is no exact answer in each situation, but there are a few things to bear in mind.

Moose, bear, mule deer, and most forest game have rather poor eyesight. Mountain and plains game—goats, sheep, and antelope—have excellent eyesight at all ranges. But all game is very sensitive to movement. If you remain still, the animal will probably not bolt if it doesn't get your scent. So you freeze in order to keep the animal where it is or in the hope that it will come closer. But now you must move your weapon or camera to take the shot.

Surprising as it may seem, you can often move so that the animal seems unaware of the motion. It is nerve-racking to bring rifle or camera into position in slow motion while a game animal is staring right at you, but it can be done. One old-timer tells how: "If the buck or moose is looking right at me, I wait a while, hoping he'll put his head down to feed or that he'll turn his head away. If he doesn't, and it looks like he'll stay put, I bring my rifle up so slowly that I can't see my arms moving." Practice that sometime for an exercise in control.

This slow movement is especially important to archers and photographers. A rifleman or a shotgunner can hope to get off a going-away shot even if the animal does come unstuck. The archer finds it very difficult to shoot accurately that fast, and the photographer is seldom interested in an animal's departing rump. Deer are so very fast, for instance, that they often "jump the string." That is, they get out of the way in the slight time interval from the twang of the bowstring to the instant when the arrow arrives where the buck *was;* so many archers use string silencers—rubber buttons slipped on the bowstring that deaden the twang of the string. Many Indians used tufts of feathers for the same purpose.

WAYS TO IMPROVE NIGHT VISION

Sometimes hunters travel at night, and some hunters—coon hunters, for instance—operate at night since the animals are on the move then. Many wildlife photographers like to call varmints at night or sit up for game and take flash pictures. Many game animals and predators come readily to calling in darkness, and the sudden flash of high-speed flash equipment doesn't seem to bother them much.

Don't sit in front of the fire or a light just before you leave your tent or cabin at night. It's best to stay in a dark room for about an hour before you go. That way, your eyes accommodate to darkness before you run the risk of stepping into a hole or off a bluff.

Angle vision works in both daylight and darkness, as the Indians knew, and it's useful when you're trying to distinguish a dimly lit object or estimate range. If you're puzzled about something that you see, move your head slightly from side to side. This allows the eyes to "feel" the object, and the binocular properties of human sight seem to reach out and touch the surface of the object. Perhaps catching the object from a slightly different angle brings out its outline more clearly. When pinpointing a coon high in a tree at night or estimating the range for a long shot at big game in daylight, the intervening objects seem to move as your head moves from side to side. Of course the twigs or other objects that are closest to the observer seem to move the most, and as distance increases away from him, they seem to move less. This illusion enables a human being to estimate distance more accurately. To the unmoving eye, the foreground, middle ground, and background sometimes seem to have no depth at all. Range estimation then is very difficult.

How to Acquire "Owl Eye"

What the Indians sometimes called "owl eye" is achieved by cupping the fingers around each eye so that dim light surrounding a distant object is concentrated in the observer's eyes and distracting light reflected from other objects is excluded. The effect of the concentration is so great that the observed object often seems to increase in size. Owl eye is especially useful at dawn and dusk when light is diffused by dampness.

Resting the Eyes

When your eyes become blurred from gazing too long in the dark or dim light, close them slowly and keep them closed for several minutes. Then open them again very slowly. If that doesn't work, keep your eyes closed while you count slowly to twenty. Then open them and try blinking again. If that does not clear your night vision, you are probably overtired or eyesore, and it is best to return to camp and take a rest.

Silhouette Vision

Indian hunters used silhouette vision to great advantage at night. It's often possible to take up a position so that you focus a dimly seen object against the skyline or against the comparatively luminous glow of a lake or wide river. You can also determine the outline of a distant object by moving it across the stars or moon. When the object blots out light as your eyes move, you get a clearer outline. If the object itself is moving, you can keep track of it by remaining still and watching the stars blink out and then on again as the object obscures the light. If you develop this skill, you'll be able to say exactly what a moving animal is—bear, moose, antelope, coyote, wolf, fox, and so forth.

THE SECRETS OF SUCCESSFUL CALLING

Hunters must spend a lot of time listening carefully to the sounds of game if they want to be successful callers, as one experienced guide on the shore of Chesapeake Bay well knew. One day the guide and a partner were sitting in a duck blind. It was a calm, quiet day, and ducks were going over at an elevation appropriate to transatlantic jets. The hunters had a good decoy rig out, but it seemed hopeless to expect a shot. Finally, one pair of black ducks came down out of the north. They were low enough, but they seemed to be about a mile away. The guide's partner whipped his wooden duck call out of his pocket and sucked in air in preparation for a mighty series of quacks.

The old-timer grabbed his companion's arm before the latter could blow and shook his head. Then he made a most astonishing noise with his mouth—*heek-heek, heek-heek,* he called, high-pitched and slightly plaintive like a split clarinet reed. The pair of blacks wavered and swung around into the hunters' rig. Two shotgun shells later, the two sportsmen had the makings of a fine meal.

"Fred," said the guide's partner, "that didn't sound any more like a black duck than a fog horn. What were you trying to imitate?"

The old-timer only glanced at his fellow-hunter oddly for an instant while the Labrador retrieved the birds. Then he revealed the secret of his success. "Son," he said, "I was imitating a drake black duck—

which you likely never listened to before. The hen blacks sound off and quack, quack just like most ducks on a farm pond, but the drake, he makes the sound I made. I saw you puffing up to blow those loud highball quacks, and I don't think the ducks would have come to that. The season's been open for a while now, and everybody's been quacking at those blacks from here to Hudson Bay. Most people think the black goes quack because that's all they ever really hear. Now you *really* listen to a flock some time when you get the chance, and then you'll hear the drakes going *heek-heek,* just like me. The birds don't hear hunters calling like that so often; so they'll come to it."

This wily guide could recognize ducks at a great distance from the blind and then make the appropriate calls in time to bring them in. His big spread of mixed geese and duck decoys helped too, of course.

Good Indian callers had similar skills, and many northern Indians still show astonishing ability to get birds when less-experienced white guides fail. The northern Crees of Canada take a big toll of Canada geese by calling them to crude brush blinds built on shore. These Crees are so expert that they call high-flying flocks of wily Canada geese to their shotguns by barking out *ee-ronk, ee-ronk, ee-ronk* with mouth and throat. When you hear Canadas "barking," you'll wonder how a human throat and mouth can produce the same noise.

Calling waterfowl was an art among the Indians long before the white man arrived in North America. Until about thirty years ago, few white men tried to call birds or animals, except, of course, those moose callers who learned from the Indians to use the birchbark horn and those few hunters who lived in areas where the turkey was still abundant. Nowadays, calling has become very popular, and a wide variety of manufactured calls is available.

This book includes information on calling each kind of animal or bird (covered later) provided that the animal or bird does respond to calls, but there are certain more general principles behind good calling that will·be discussed here.

Learning Animal Communication Systems

To call well, you must have some idea of the means of communication used by birds and animals. From the chickadee to the moose, birds and animals communicate with each other in one way or another. As hunters who have listened to them carefully know, some wild creatures carry on conversations, accented for emotion as well as meaning.

Squirrels that chatter and chase up and down tree trunks and scamper madly over the rustling leaves, pausing from time to time with menace or "follow me" on their expressive faces, are not just romping. They are communicating. Male squirrels confront each other for a moment and communicate by definite signs. One animal retreats. The pursuer is then recognized as the master of the other and has first choice of available food and females.

Foxes, wolves, and some other animals mark their regular runways by urinating on stones, trees, and boulders to attract or warn off others of their kind by means of scent. The beaver perfumes clay and mud patties with his glandular castor scent to attract females. Mink use their musk glands to communicate, and male cottontail rabbits leave signs of their presence by rubbing their chins on a stump or tree. Few woodsmen can ignore the devastating scent left by a wolverine that forces its way into a cabin. Even snakes leave scent trails and follow others that interest them.

Sometimes a hunter calls perfectly, knowing that the quarry is nearby, but gets no response. It is often his scent that disturbs the animal, or it may be an alarming scent from another animal. Indians have long known that the sounds made by animals and birds are only one part of the entire communication pattern, and that a hunter's call must fit in with it. Indians would never attempt, for instance, to call in a wild turkey if a red-tailed hawk or other large predatory bird were circling overhead.

Hoofed animals paw the ground, stamp their feet, and snort to signal impatience or anger and to warn off an intruder. The bellow of a moose or the belling of an elk conveys two meanings—the search for a mate and a challenge to fight other males. These animals also communicate with each other by rattling their antlers against trees, branches, or bushes. Whitetail deer and antelope communicate with their flashing flags and rumps. When a deer's flag goes up or a pronghorn's rump hairs stand erect and flash white, the animal is warning that danger is present. When you see those signals, it's almost always useless to try a stalk. Beaver and muskrats communicate

Beaver

Mink

by diving into the water with a warning splash. The beaver also slaps the water with his flat tail to signal danger.

Calling Birds

Any novice hunter learning to communicate with crows soon discovers that the birds have several distinct calls with definite variations in rhythm and loudness. Each one has a definite meaning. This is evident when a novice crow caller sounds the alarm call instead of the rally call. Grackles communicate through their calls and chatter, but they also signal with eyes, beak, head, wings, and tail.

When calling most birds, one is always right to give the signature call of the species in order to arouse interest and inform the bird that others of its kind are within hearing. During the breeding season, male songbirds perch and sing. The male bird does not sing out of sheer joy. The songs are territorial signals, warning off other male birds of its own kind and notifying other intruders that the singer has established his boundaries. The calls also attract the female. If you imitate the territorial song or call of a songbird, the male bird often comes quickly to investigate or even to attack the intruder, and you may attract a female. That's the time when you may get an interesting photograph, and it's a good way to draw small birds out of thick cover where photography is difficult.

A low, unspecific warbling or whistling sometimes has a similar effect, and it may attract females as well as males during the breeding season and afterward. One mechanical call consists of two disks that rub against each other when they are rotated. The resulting squeaks and warbles sound like no particular bird, but they arouse curiosity. Many birds respond either by singing or coming to investigate. If you can recognize the various responses, you can locate the various species. Indians often whistled and warbled in this way to call in predatory birds and animals that hoped to prey on nestlings.

Many birds are known by names based on their calls; for instance, the kildeer, a big plover, calls *kill-dee, kill-dee,* usually when in flight, and the bob-white's name is based on its signature call. Going through a standard bird guide and checking the names of the birds against the notations on the sounds they make will give you a large vocabulary of calls. You may already know the names and appearance of many birds. If you find that the name is based on the sound the bird makes, you are adding greatly to your knowledge.

Types of Calling

There are three general types of calling. In one of them, the caller imitates the sounds made by the bird or animal that he wishes to attract. In calling predators, the caller most often imitates the calls of the prey. For instance, the most popular call for foxes, coyotes, and birds of prey is the sound of a dying rabbit. A third type of calling depends on making noises that simply arouse curiosity. The Indians depended on these curiosity calls, and by experience, learned that low tapping, scratching, quiet and indistinct whistling, or blowing on a wide blade of grass or a leaf held between the base and tip of the thumbs, as shown in the drawing, often works. This type of quiet calling is often effective when the caller really does not know what kind of bird or animal to expect. The sounds are not human, but they represent no specific animal or bird.

The sounds made by the predators themselves can sometimes be used to advantage. The Indians often imitated the call of a hunting hawk to freeze quail, squirrels, rabbits, and other small game so that they would stay still long enough for an easy shot with a bow.

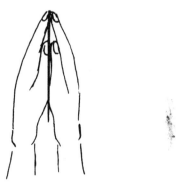

Holding Leaf in Position for Calling

Indian and Eskimo callers were often more successful than white men because the natives had an astonishing range of vocal sounds in their languages that the white caller found it very difficult to imitate. These sounds were often used to decoy animals and birds.

The Salish hunters of the Northwest Coast could place a stiff leaf between the teeth and blow on it to imitate the bleat of a fawn—a sure call for wolves, wildcats, and other predators as well as does and even bucks. The Salish hunters also made effective calling devices for moose and elk from the hollow stalks of sunflowers and hollow bones.

Good Indian callers could keep up a regular conversation with the quarry. They often called from blinds or thick cover, but if the game would not come to the blind, the hunter would leave it and stalk the animal, meanwhile keeping up the animal's interest with intermittent calling. Of course, the volume of the call had to be reduced as the hunter and the game came closer and closer together.

Manufactured Calls

Modern manufactured calls are available for almost every purpose, and their complexity and prices vary greatly too. For a beginner, a hard-rubber, mouth-operated call is satisfactory since he doesn't have the necessary skills to use the finely made hardwood calls. With mouth-operated calling devices, the instrument should incorporate some means of varying the pitch. If the call is capable of only one pitch, there's no possibility of adjusting it higher or lower if you find that the single pitch is off.

When mouth-operated calls are used in cold weather, saliva often enters them and freezes, silencing the call or altering the pitch. Moisture from the breath may also accumulate and freeze. Most good calling devices can be taken apart and wiped free of moisture. Calling devices that operate with vibrating reeds should be easy to take apart so that the reed can be cleaned and dried or replaced. If the call is a one-piece device, blow into it backwards from time to time to clear out moisture. It's best to carry two calls on a hunting trip. If one freezes or clogs, the other is ready.

Some calling devices depend on friction to make the sounds. Typical of this type are the cedar-box calls used for turkeys. These devices require the use of two hands, and make it difficult to hold a camera or a gun. Some calling devices are operated by squeezing a rubber bulb to force air through a reed. A few hunters do not squeeze these calls with their fingers. Instead, they place them under a foot or a knee and gently squeeze the bulb that way, leaving both hands free. Mouth-operated calls should be light enough so that they can be held in the mouth without the use of the hands. A lanyard loop around the neck helps when you drop the call out of your mouth to use binoculars, camera, or weapon. Some calling devices can be inserted entirely inside the mouth. One turkey call consists of a vibrating diaphragm that is pushed up against the roof of the mouth and blown. It's very popular with archers, who usually like to have both hands free to keep an arrow on the string.

How to Use Game-calling Records

The best way to learn to call is to listen to the game itself until you can imitate the sounds either with mouth and throat or a calling device. The various game-calling records now on the market are a great help. There are two kinds. One type is intended to call in the game when used with a battery-operated portable loudspeaker. The law in most jurisdictions now forbids the use of electronic devices to call game animals and birds; so these records are useless for the purpose originally intended. Loudspeakers and records for game calling are legal in most jurisdictions only when used to call varmints or destructive birds not protected by law. For instance, most states and provinces allow hunters to use loudspeakers to call crows.

The other type of record includes instruction by an experienced caller. As a rule, the instructor tells the novice how to call in various situations and then gives samples.

Sit down with your record player and listen. Don't touch an artificial call until you are sure that the correct sound is imprinted in your mind. Then practice imitating it until you believe you are hitting the right notes with the right rhythm, and have the various sequences correct. Then test your calling ability even if the hunting season isn't open. Try to locate a game farm or hunting preserve that raises or stocks the type of game you plan to hunt or photograph. Usually, the owners won't object if you try out your calling on penned birds or half-wild game, and often you'll be able to listen to the game it-self. Always ask permission first.

You may be preparing for a trip to hunt a wild animal that isn't present where you live. Visiting a game farm or hunting preserve allows you to hear and imitate the sounds the animal makes long before it's time to leave. In New York State, for instance, one large game farm stocks elk. If you visit it during the rut, you'll get your calling in shape before going on that western elk hunt. Bird sanctuaries are excellent places to study the calls of game birds and songbirds, but make sure the authorities or the keeper have no objection before you begin your imitations.

A record played indoors often differs from the natural sound made outdoors. It's sometimes very revealing to take the record player outside and listen in the open. You may be amazed at the difference in tone, something that you should take into account in your imitation.

Some mouth-operated calls are intended to amplify sounds that the caller makes with his vocal cords and tongue. Many waterfowl calls are made in this way, and the manufacturer should state that fact in his printed instructions. When using this type of call, you must imitate the record or the natural sound perfectly with your throat and mouth. The call only increases the volume of the sound.

SCENT

How to Eliminate Human Odors

Many Indian tribesmen took ritual baths in order to cleanse themselves before hunting. Some of them even spent long periods in steam baths made by plunging red-hot stones into water in dugouts. The Indians believed that this cleansing of the flesh made them more acceptable to the gods and that hunting success would be granted. The elimination of the sour human odor that is easily detected by game was probably more important, however. Indian hunters did not smoke or eat while on stand or stillhunting because the odor of tobacco and food is alarming to most game animals, though they may not connect it with man.

Some modern hunters who must come close to the game imitate the

Indians in this and will not bring their deer-hunting clothes into the house. They believe that the clothes would pick up the thick indoor odors inside. The Indian's rule still stands; it's not wise to smoke a cigar, pipe, or cigarette on deer stand or break out a salami sandwich if you're waiting for a fox or coyote.

Scent Clues That Animals Leave Behind

The human nose is not a precise instrument, and few hunters claim that they use it to find game, but sometimes it does work. In heavy cover, you may catch a whiff of the very distinctive smell given off by elk. The odor of rotting meat after a bear, a mountain lion, or some other predator has made a kill sometimes leads a hunter to a productive area. The urine of most game animals has a very powerful, acrid smell, and Indians could sometimes locate a big moose by first catching the odor of its urine and then seeing the tracks.

Fresh-spilled blood has a distinct, sweetish, almost overwhelming smell. You may smell blood after a shot at a big-game animal before you actually see it. A fleeing wounded animal often lies down to try to regain its strength, and in its terror, it usually urinates freely. If you are tracking a wounded animal and catch the combined odor of fresh blood and acrid urine, you may be close to your quarry.

Men who live a great deal of their lives outdoors are much more adept at using the sense of smell to hunt than the average city dweller. In the city, the smells of gasoline, motor exhaust, millions of people, cooking, and all sorts of manufacturing processes blunt a human being's sense of smell. In clean air, it is possible to smell many animal odors, and some big-game kills have been made because the hunter smelled the animal even before he saw it or its tracks.

Scent Lures for Game

Indian hunters sometimes used female deer scent made from the glands to attract buck deer, and concentrated deer scent is available in bottled form today. Trappers also use artificial and natural concentrates to attract animals to their sets. For instance, professional predator trappers working for the government often keep coyotes captive to collect urine for use on their traps.

How game scents attract animals is something of a mystery. Sometimes they work, and sometimes they don't. Female deer scent of the animal in heat sometimes attracts buck deer during the rut. If the buck is not breeding any longer, he may lose his caution when he smells the scent on the hunter's clothes because he believes that he is dealing only with a harmless doe. And that may be the secret of animal scents. When the hunter sprinkles his clothes, particularly his boots, with them, it masks the human smell and the smell of cooked foods and tobacco. One western hunter used to douse himself with buck lure before going after Columbia blacktail deer. He once was sitting in a clump of brush when he was amazed to see a coyote coming in from downwind. Normally, a coyote would never approach a man from that direction, but this one did, and the hunter shot him. Presumably, the coyote was investigating the enticing scent of doe deer in hopes of picking up an injured animal and never caught the masked human scent. Varmint hunters may be missing a good bet by not masking their own odors when calling. However, only a few men have tried it, and their results were not conclusive.

AIMING FOR THE VITAL AREAS OF GAME

Most novice hunters have very little idea of the anatomy of animals and therefore they do not place their shots properly. The best possible training, of course, is to skin and cut up game animals or help someone do it as Indian youngsters did.

Four-footed Animals

The placement of the heart and lungs of four-footed animals is quite low in the chest. Not knowing this, many hunters place their shots too high. From the side, the total lung-heart area of a deer is only about 10 inches high and about 14 inches long—a small target at 200 or more yards, and a very small target for the archer at almost any range.

As shown in the drawing, the line formed by the rear of the upper leg cuts the heart-lung area in half when viewed from the side. Placing a bullet or an arrow on that line at just the right height may pierce the lung on your side, the upper part of the heart, and the lung on the other side. Most hunters describe this shot as hitting just "behind the shoulder." The use of the word "shoulder" is deceptive. It gives the impression that the vital area is high in the chest because most people think in terms of human anatomy. Almost all four-footed animals have the vital organs in the lower two-thirds of the body. If you are a little high with a rifle, you may smash the spine above the lungs, but that's hard to hit and it's easy to shoot high over the animal's back.

Bears

The heart-lung area is the preferred target with all North American game except bears. Hit in the heart or the lungs or both, most animals will go down immediately or run only a very short distance. A grizzly bear, a big Alaska brown, a polar bear, or even a big black bear, however, seems to have a lot more stamina than most other animals, especially if the bear has been angered or superficially wounded. Many a hunter has put a heavy enough bullet in a grizzly's heart only to find that the bear could still run 100 yards or more. Even with a bullet directly through the heart, an angry bear may charge and severely maul the hunter.

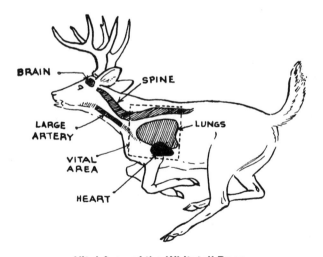

Vital Area of the Whitetail Deer

After the Indians acquired firearms, they soon learned to "break the bear down" by hitting him in the upper shoulders. With the grizzly, brown, and polar bear, the target is the lower part of the big hump over the forelegs. A good hit there from the side breaks both shoulder blades, and the bear cannot move his forelegs. If you shoot a little high, you may shatter the spine. The bullet should be placed in line with the middle of the shoulder—not behind the shoulder as with nondangerous game. When hunting a black bear, sight right on the middle of the body, a little high. Blacks do not have conspicuous humps. A second shot in the heart-lung area, the neck, or the head finishes the job, though most modern trophy hunters avoid firing at a bear's head since they like to have that part of the animal in perfect trophy condition.

It is extremely unwise to fire at any bear directly from the rear, and if you have a frontal shot, it's often best to hold on the bulge of either shoulder to cripple the bear. When the range is very close, hold on the front of the skull. If you are low and the bear is high, aim at the point of the jaw or the open mouth to shatter the entire brain pan. If you hit with the right bullet, you'll stop him in his tracks.

Going-away Shots

It is rare to find a wary game animal standing still broadside to the hunter. Most often, game animals are going away from the hunter, and that fact poses something of a problem, particularly for archers. If a deer, elk, antelope, or other nondangerous game runs straight away from the hunter, he·has only two possible targets. He can aim at the neck (including the back of the head), intending to kill by cutting or smashing the spinal column or the brain, or he can aim directly between the hams, fairly high, to drive the bullet right through the intestinal tract and into the heart-lung area. Both are difficult shots even for a skilled hunter firing an accurate, high-powered rifle.

Limitations of Archery Tackle

Chiefly because of the small target area, both of these shots from the rear are almost impossible for the archer. Most experienced archers who know the limitations of bow and arrow and who are good sportsmen pass up every shot that must be taken directly from the rear, because it results in so much wounded game.

The archer does have a good shot if the animal's rump is presented at a slight angle. In fact, many archers prefer to angle the arrow into the animal just behind the ribs so that it ranges forward into the heart-lung area from the rear, inside the ribs. A precisely placed shaft touches no bone from that angle. If the animal is facing away at a fairly acute angle, and the archer holds just in front of the swell of the haunch, his target is comparatively large, and hemorrhage caused by the broadhead may involve both lungs and heart. Piercing one of these organs will kill fairly rapidly.

There is little or no shocking power to an arrow even when shot from a hunting bow with a 60- or 70-pound pull. An arrow kills by causing bleeding, especially when the broadhead happens to cut a vital organ. By contrast, a .30/06 rifle bullet at 100 yards hits with about 2,400 foot-pounds of energy. A rifleman who switches to archery tackle sometimes has difficulty in realizing its limitations—something that the Indian knew from childhood.

The vast majority of big game killed with arrows dies by bleeding alone. For this reason, the archer has a heavy obligation to place his shots very carefully. Riflemen and those who hunt deer with shotguns have the same obligation.

Shots from in Front

When hunting nondangerous game from directly in front, the best target is the lower chest. If you're a little high, but centered, an arrow will go into the lower throat and will probably kill fairly quickly. If you're dead on, the animal will be hit in the heart; if you're slightly to one side, one lung will be affected. The same aiming points work well with a rifle.

An archer who faces big game from the front or at a slight quartering angle is in a dangerous position. It can be difficult to down a charging bear or an angry moose even with a rifle. This is why many responsible big-game hunters who use bows recommend a back-up gun—another hunter or a guide armed with a heavy rifle who intervenes if the situation becomes too dangerous. Foolish bravado with archery tackle may result in a mauling or death. This is why Indian archers either left big bears alone or only took sure shots.

Indian archers were experts at placing their arrows correctly because there was enough game to provide them with almost unlimited practice. Lately, modern archers are turning to three-dimensional, animal-shaped targets made of foam plastic. Try hitting vital areas on these targets from every angle except directly from the rear, and you'll learn how accurate effective bow-and-arrow work must be.

Shooting from Elevated Stands

When shooting from an elevated stand in a tree or on a steep hillside, the best target is usually the middle of the back when using firearms. Try to angle your shot downward toward the heart-lung area. If you are slightly forward of the animal, aim right at the top of the shoulders. From the side, angle in just to the near side of the spine. All these shots make a humane kill if you are using an adequate rifle, and if the shot can be centered, you may smash the backbone before the bullet even reaches heart or lung.

Good archers aim slightly to the side of the spine when shooting from above because an arrow from a powerful bow can be depended on to drive between or through the upper ribs and penetrate the heart-lung area. The spine itself is too tough.

The archer should always have another shaft ready after the first shot. If at all possible, get off a second shaft before the animal can run. A quiver mounted on the bow helps, but holding the second arrow in the bow hand parallel to the bow works well too, provided you practice using it enough so that it doesn't throw your shooting style off. Many archers stick their second broadheaded arrow into soft ground when they are shooting from a stand at ground level. It can be picked up quickly by the nock. Broadheads should be very sharp, and an arrow that has been stuck into rocky or sandy ground has lost its sharp edges even before it is nocked. Carry a file and a small honing stone on bowhunting trips and go over the edges of every arrow you recover after a shot. If a broadhead is shot into brush and recovered, one or more of the edges are usually dulled.

No sporting firearms hunter or archer ever aims for a game

animal's paunch. A hit there does not kill, and it usually does not cause much bleeding. Instead, the intestines or the stomach are pierced, and the animal may die in agony miles away.

FOLLOWING UP WOUNDED GAME

A hunter who connects when he fires usually knows it. A high-powered rifle bullet hitting a game animal makes a distinctive *thwock* that can be heard at a considerable distance. The archer's eyes follow his arrow in flight and may even see it hit and penetrate. Even the shotgunner using buckshot and the handgunner with his low-powered cartridge often hear the impact, and the animal flinches when hit, drops right in its tracks, or is knocked off its feet.

If the animal went down, the tribal hunter did not yell or run toward the game. He got another arrow nocked as quickly as possible. He remained perfectly still and watched the game for signs of life. Many an animal has been lost because a modern hunter did not follow the Indian's example. Often, a big-game animal is stunned by a glancing or superficial hit. The big buck, bear, moose or other heavy animal goes down, seemingly dead, and the hunter runs forward with his weapon carelessly held. Then the animal jumps up and bolts, presenting the hunter with a difficult shot for which he is unprepared. Wait several minutes before you walk up to the game, and then move slowly with your weapon ready.

Avoiding Injury from Wounded Animals

Approach all "dead" game with caution. The stories of careless deer hunters mutilated on the antlers of seemingly dead deer are legion, and many other animals are dangerous when wounded. Even the inoffensive pronghorn antelope can injure a man severely with his sharp hoofs if he kicks convulsively just as the hunter bends over the motionless animal or kneels down beside it. The safest approach is from the animal's back as it lies on the ground. In some cases, the nature of the wound is quite conclusive. A solid hit in a vital area or a dislocated or shattered spine is usually apparent to the eye, but take no chances. Gently touch the animal's eye with the muzzle of your gun or the tip of an arrow. Even an unconscious animal will blink if it is still alive. If the animal does blink, put another bullet into it or use another broadhead.

If you are anxious to save meat, the neck just below the skull is a good place for a finishing shot with firearm or bow, but that mars the animal's cape for purposes of taxidermy. Some hunters cut the throat of every big game animal that they put down in order to make sure that it is dead and bleed it, but that mars the cape too. If you want a head-and-neck mount, it's probably best to put another bullet or arrow into the heart-lung area.

Following up a wounded game animal is a difficult and sometimes dangerous task, especially if you have shot the animal in rough country just before sunset. Good sportsmanship demands a quick, merciful kill. In addition, you'll avoid a lot of troublesome tracking if you shoot well enough to anchor the animal.

Every time a humane hunter fires a shot, he investigates the results even if he believes that he has missed. Game is too scarce today to be wasted, and even in frontier times, Indians and white men valued wild meat and hides too much to waste an animal.

Before making any move to follow a wounded animal, take a few minutes to look at the lay of the land and think about the nature of the hit. You may save yourself hours of difficult, perhaps dangerous tracking by figuring out where the animal is likely to go.

Look for blood on the ground, grass, or leaves, and don't give up until you have followed the animal's tracks or general line of flight for a considerable distance. If the animal has gotten into thick cover, and you can't see a clear blood trail or tracks, it often pays to zigzag back and forth as you follow its general direction.

Following Blood Trails

If you find a great deal of bright red blood and perhaps bits of shattered bone, you have made a good hit, and you may have cut an artery. The animal will probably drop in a short distance, and you'll have little trouble recovering it. If you find very dark blood, you have missed vital arteries, and unless you have shattered a joint, the animal will probably travel quite a distance. If you discover a few dark spots and a great deal of watery, yellowish fluid, you have hit the animal in the paunch, and it is losing intestinal fluid and perhaps urine. A hit there usually means a long, difficult tracking job, but if you're a good sportsman, you'll follow up as long as possible in order to put the animal out of its misery.

If it's possible to get help from friends, by all means do so. One man following the tracks directly and two flankers out to the sides to catch the animal if it turns and makes an effort to circle back make an effective team, provided all the trackers are experienced enough to move silently and slowly. If there's a good strike dog in camp or among the pack, that's the time to use him, provided it's legal to use dogs in your area for the game you are trying to track down. It's easy for a good hound to run down a wounded animal. The scent is fresh and the scent of blood or intestinal fluids is easy to follow.

If you're following a wounded moose, bear, or other dangerous game, be very careful. Even a small buck deer sometimes charges the hunter if he's wounded and cornered or so enraged that he loses all natural fear. A bear bedded down and licking a wound is hard to see, if the animal moves slightly aside from its straight track.

There's a good deal of argument among hunters about whether or not it is wise to follow up a wounded animal immediately. Some hunters will tell you that it's best to sit down for at least the time it takes to smoke a cigarette before following a blood trail. The theory is that the animal will lie down to rest after going a short distance and that the wound will stiffen up and either make it impossible for the animal to go on or slow it down so much that catching up will be easy. That works well if the wound has been serious, but sometimes it doesn't work with a paunch hit. Even if this wound does stiffen up, it doesn't interfere seriously with the animal's legs and shoulders, and it may keep on.

Each hunter must decide what to do next, depending on what he saw when he fired and what blood, bone, or cut hair he finds. Broadheaded arrows and bullets usually cut a lot of hair when they hit, and almost all game animals have light-colored throats and undersides and dark upper bodies. After a shot at a deer, for instance, a great deal of white hair indicates a low hit. Yellow body fluid with it means a hit in the paunch.

In some heavily hunted areas, you'll lose your buck without an immediate follow-up. If you keep the animal moving, you'll often run it into other hunters, and in the eastern states at least, the man who finally puts the animal down is the one who keeps the meat. That is why many eastern hunters follow up right away even if they think the animal might lie down and stiffen up in a fairly short time. This works out well enough. The hunter will either catch up and put the animal down for good or he will run it into other hunters who will do the job for him. Either way, the animal's suffering is ended. In a wilderness area where hunters are scarce, a long tracking job is common if you wound.

If nightfall is coming on, it may be best to wait until morning before following up wounded game, and you may be obliged to do so if the law forbids hunting at night and even forbids the tracking of a wounded animal. Tracking on a dark night is impossible in any case. Even wounded game animals feel more secure in darkness, and the animal may lie down and stiffen or even die before morning. If you're a good enough tracker, you'll probably be able to find it. If rain or snow threatens late in the day, it's probably best to follow up as long as the light lasts since snow will cover all tracks, and heavy rain obliterates all signs.

Where Wounded Game Heads

In hilly country, most wounded animals will go downhill. They will also head for water if they can make it in order to drink because loss of body fluid causes a terrible thirst. Sometimes you can locate a wounded animal by going downhill to the nearest creek or stream and walking the bank on the near side. If the bank is muddy or sandy, it's easy to locate tracks.

6 /

The Art of Becoming Invisible

MAN HAS ALWAYS used concealment to hunt animals and birds, and in recent years, nature observers and photographers have been using the hunter's techniques of concealment by building blinds. Blinds may be built with natural materials such as brush, reeds, branches, or grass or they may be merely pits dug in the ground.

TECHNIQUES OF CONCEALMENT

An elaborate blind isn't always needed. Instead, the hunter may take advantage of natural cover such as reeds or brush. "Hides"—a term used in England—are used by many hunters who must move around because they cannot expect the game they await to show up near a permanent structure. Outdoorsmen who live where game is so abundant that an elaborate blind is not needed use similar temporary, often portable, hides. In Alaska and the Canadian North, few Indians and Eskimos build complicated, permanent blinds. These hunters more often pile up a rough semicircle of ice and snow or force evergreen boughs into the ground when hunting waterfowl. Elaborate waterfowl blinds are used farther south where the migrating birds follow specific flyways and are more wary after encountering many hunters on the flight south.

Camouflage

If the hunter, photographer, or nature observer must move about a great deal, he often attaches natural or artificial camouflage to his clothing, and uses dark makeup or a face net to conceal the white of hands and face. Much scientific effort has been expended to develop effective multicolor camouflage. The chief function of camouflage clothing is to break up a man's outline. Various combinations of colors are used in blotches and whorls to match the background colors of foliage or ground, but merely matching background is not enough. The garment must camouflage the man's outline so that parts of him seem to merge with the background. Modern camouflage—originally developed to deceive the human eye—has proved effective in stalking many animals and birds.

Two new developments are camouflage with a great deal of green against a dull background along with brown tones, and another which employs whorls and splotches of red along with a little green and brown. The first is said to be especially useful in evergreen cover and was developed for hunting in green forests and jungles. The latter, though clearly visible to another man, does not spook deer. This bright pattern is safer during the firearms hunting season.

The Importance of Hiding Hands and Face

Indian hunters relied more on hides and clever concealment than they did on any form of blind or camouflage. You often see a white man afield at a distance as three white dots when he is wearing dull clothing. Face and hands stand out vividly. A good outdoorsman knows that his chief problem in a blind or when using camouflage is to conceal his human form. The white of hands and face and, at close range, the contrast between the white of the eye and the dark pupil are the chief giveaways. Waterfowl hunters almost always keep their faces hidden until the last moment before shooting, and turkey hunters favor face nets or dark makeup.

Breaking Up the Human Outline

Indians often decorated their bows with colorful designs and often painted their faces and bodies with decorative patterns. At close range, these patterns showed up clearly, especially when very bright paint was used, but at longer range these bright patterns were difficult to pick out. Bright colors break up the human outline, and since the Indian did not show white hands and face, he was well concealed in his paint.

There is a lesson here for the modern hunter. Unless you are hunting or photographing color-sensitive game such as wild turkeys and waterfowl, your outline is more important than the colors you use. Bulky, loose clothing is better than well-fitting, tighter clothing.

How Movement Alarms Game

To most game animals and birds, movement is much more noticeable than color. A careless gesture or a nervous shifting of the leg on deer stand will often spook an oncoming buck. Indians seldom used branches or leaves tied to the headdress or body, since leafy branches sway and accentuate movement. A nod of the head that would go unnoticed by the game is exaggerated when the branches move. The branches or twigs also increase the height of the hunter. It's difficult to keep low with several inches of foliage sticking up over your head and shoulders. Good hunters know that they should look around a boulder, a hummock, or a log—not over them—and that is harder to do with leafy camouflage on head and shoulders.

Camouflage is of little concern to those who hunt big game with firearms. In most states and provinces, the law requires the firearms hunter to wear bright clothing during the big-game season. The waterfowler, varmint hunter, bowhunter, and photographer, on the other hand, use camouflage a great deal.

Preventing Reflection from Weapons and Cameras

The light-reflecting surfaces of fiberglass bows and arrow shafts spook game too, and even the light reflecting off the edges of a broadheaded arrow can do the same. Indian equipment was dull in finish and did not reflect light. Many bowhunters use neutral-colored bow socks that fit over the entire bow. Bow socks are often made of dull-green cloth because green leaves are still on the trees. Another method is to paint the bow itself in green, brown, and tan blotches.

Many bowhunters hesitate to paint an expensive bow; so they cover it with masking tape and paint on that surface. Still others wrap their bows with colored camouflage tape.

Broadheaded arrows for big game are often carried in an open-sided quiver attached to the belt, a strap over the shoulder, or the bow itself. These open-sided quivers rack the arrows tightly with clamps, but the hunter can pull out an arrow with ease. These new quivers are excellent for hunting, but they do allow the fletching and the light-reflecting shafts to show. The best solution is to use dull shafts and fletching.

The shotgunner or rifleman who goes after varmints and wild turkey has much the same problem. Light shining off a gun barrel or polished stock is enough to spook an approaching fox or a wary turkey. An old gun with a dull barrel and a scratched stock is better for varmints or turkey than a bright new weapon. The smooth-bore muskets used by Indian hunters were often rusty and badly scratched, but they were not conspicuous in the woods. Some varmint hunters paint or tape their weapons to camouflage them, but care must be taken not to jam the action with paint or the gum on the tape. Photographers have a problem with the bright gear they carry. A few go over their cameras carefully with dull paint to camouflage light-reflecting surfaces.

Special Camouflage for Special Terrain

Bowhunting, varmint shooting, and camera work on the snow call for white clothing and white equipment. Some Eskimo and other hunters sew white cloth inside their camouflage jackets, pants, and soft hats so that the garments can be reversed if there is a sudden fall of snow.

Camouflage outfits can be simple and easy to make, provided the hunter uses his imagination. In the western United States, open seasons have recently been declared on the lesser sandhill crane, a big bird that was often hunted by the Plains Indians. These birds had not been hunted for forty or fifty years, and yet good hunters quickly adapted to the game. The birds are found in open country, often near water. Blinds constructed of brush and grass are too obvious, and the birds flare away when they are used. Soon, a few good hunters found the answer—burlap sacking sewn onto a blanket to which dry grass is sewn. The hunter covers himself with the grass-sewn blanket and watches for birds through a small slit, gun in hand, until a flock flies in to the silhouette decoys around him. Then he throws off the blanket, gets up on one knee, and shoots. Imagination can develop good camouflage for almost any situation.

BLINDS

Some blinds which conceal the hunter from game are obvious to the human eye. For instance, in southern Ontario and Quebec, the outbuildings of abandoned farmsteads are often used as blinds in bear and deer hunting. To a human being, the old shed or smokehouse is conspicuous, but to the black bear or whitetail coming to feed on fallen apples, the weathered wooden structure has become a part of the landscape. The open-water reef blinds used for waterfowl in North Carolina on salt water are big structures based on four heavy pilings driven into the sand or mud, and often the box on top in which the hunters sit is made of bare planks. Grass and reeds are not used to conceal the structure. A man can spot this kind of reef blind miles away, and so can geese and ducks, but these blinds are permanent structures, and even migrating waterfowl soon become used to them. When the hunter or photographer puts out decoys and calls enticingly, the birds come right in. It is important, whenever possible, to introduce any kind of blind to the game long before shooting or photography is to take place. If a blind must be constructed quickly and used almost right away, it must fit in with the natural surroundings as well as possible, and that is sometimes difficult.

Waterfowl hunters who use permanent blinds often visit them at intervals throughout the year to keep them in good repair and make sure that they remain an unchanging, permanent part of the landscape. When the Indians built their simple blinds for turkey hunting, they let them emerge slowly out of the ground much like a natural growth by adding a few reeds or a little cut brush at a time. Modern photographers who take pictures of wary, rare birds or animals do much the same when they construct their blinds over several days or weeks. Each morning, there is only a very small change in the natural scene. The problem is to avoid frightening the whooping crane, falcon, or other rare bird or animal out of the territory. If you slash about with machete and saw to build a blind in one day, the animal or bird may be in the next county that night.

When the structure is complete, the photographer enters it before the sun rises and remains there until he gets his important pictures. The photographs of rare birds that appear in natural-history magazines are often the result of many weeks of careful blind building and patient waiting. If the photographer had disturbed the surroundings or had made too much noise, those beautiful pictures taken from a slowly constructed blind in a neighboring tree only a few yards away, would never have been possible.

Choosing a Location

The blind must be located at a place where the quarry will probably appear, and setting the blind up in the right place is more than half the job. Good bowhunters build their blinds at deer crossings, and waterfowlers place their blinds where flights of birds appear regularly. Skillful scouting and careful advance observation of the game will give you the clues to the right spot.

Materials for the blind cannot be cut right at the spot where the blind is built. If you do that, you'll disturb the surroundings too much and frighten off the game. Sometimes, it's difficult to get matching materials, but if you can do so, bring reeds, brush, grass, or other natural materials from a location that is out of sight of the place where the blind will be built, and in constructing it, disturb the site as little as possible.

Tribal hunters were experts at choosing a site where game could be expected to appear. At that point, they used natural hides such as a clump of evergreens or thick reeds. Their ability to remain still for long periods of time was a more effective means of concealment than the average blind built by modern hunters. Self-control and knowledge of territory was the Indian's method of concealing himself rather than using blinds and camouflage.

Caution in Approaching a Blind

The Indian also knew that some game is very sensitive to artificial changes in the natural scene, and was careful when approaching his hide and leaving it. If possible, he approached the blind against the wind in order not to disturb game nearby, but he also tried to use a different route each time so that he would not make a beaten path through brush or grass—something that disturbs many animals and birds. Often, we are not so careful. A good waterfowl blind is constructed, but when birds begin to fall, the hunters use the same route through reeds or grass to retrieve them. This soon beats down the growth and makes an obvious pathway that is easily seen by an approaching flight. That's one good way to make a well-constructed blind useless, because it takes a long time for the natural growth to spring up again.

Avoiding Movement in a Blind

Movement by the hunter in the blind often spooks birds and game animals, but the hunter or photographer must allow himself elbow room to move gun or camera. Since every blind must have some openings, and the quarry can usually see into the blind through them, unnecessary movement, especially abrupt motions, are to be avoided even in the best blind.

Unnatural movement of the blind itself or a part of it is also a giveaway. After you have completed your blind, back off a bit and look at it. If reeds or brush move unnaturally in the wind or if the foliage you have used is broken or looks unnatural in any other way, you're unlikely to get a shot or your pictures. Correct any defect. When hunting or waiting to take a picture, try to avoid touching the blind since you may move part of it.

Most people do not have the Indian's ability to remain motionless, and this is particularly true if the hunter or photographer is uncomfortable. In any blind, try to arrange things so that you can lie down or sit comfortably. It's not being soft to use a stool in a duck blind or place a sheet of dull-colored waterproof plastic on the ground so that you can sit or lie down without contacting dampness. The hardy Eskimo hunter often sits on a waterproof sealskin.

Camouflage Cloth

In some areas, cutting natural materials for blinds is difficult or unlawful, and they must be brought in from a distant area. Few farmers would consent to your cutting apple branches to make a deer blind on a bowhunting trip. Head for an abandoned orchard instead, and then bring the materials with you when you are setting up. If it proves impossible to get natural materials, you'll have to use a camouflage cloth or some similar material. In some surroundings, old burlap sacking or weathered brown canvas is enough. The Indians sometimes used hides that were rubbed and stained to match surrounding terrain. Fabrics are often used in temporary blinds that can be moved from place to place. The usual method is to mount the cloth on stakes or laths with staples and drive the stakes into the ground to surround the hunter or photographer with a wall of fabric. Drive the stakes in a circular or semicircular pattern. Square corners are rare in nature.

You can make a substitute for manufactured camouflage cloth by blotching old fabric with a paintbrush or spray gun. In open grassland, guy ropes are needed to anchor the blind. Use old weathered rope or cord for the guys and camouflaged pegs.

Portable Fabric Blinds

A fabric blind with attached stakes, guy ropes, and pegs is a single unit that you can roll up and move. Place the fabric flat on the ground with the guy ropes and stakes on top of the fabric; then roll it up and tie. It's possible to arrive at a promising location and set up this type of blind in a short time. If you must drive stakes and pegs, do so as quietly as possible. It's better to force the stakes and pegs into the ground when possible instead of driving them. Unnatural noises spook game too.

Blinds Made from Chicken Wire

A good blind that can be rolled up is often made of chicken wire—the older and more tarnished the better. Indians sometimes used thong or fiber netting for the same purpose. Stakes, guy ropes, and pegs are permanently attached to the wire, and grass or leafy twigs are woven into the mesh openings. If you use this type of blind, you can renew the natural materials whenever the old ones deteriorate or the blind is set up in an area where the materials already in the mesh would not look natural. When you insert stalks of grass or twigs in the mesh, weave the stems over and under several strands of wire or fiber and leave them upright, free to move naturally in the wind at about the same height as the surrounding natural growth. If you live in a fishing area, try fishing net instead of chicken wire. Fish net can be blotched to match the terrain, and sometimes fine-mesh painted netting works well enough without any vegetation in the mesh.

Waterfowl Blinds

Waterfowl hunters have developed many different kinds of blinds that work well with other kinds of birds and animals. Waterfowlers learned some of their techniques from Indian hunters, and even today, many of the locations chosen for waterfowl blinds were originally used by Indians. For instance, many good places for duck and goose blinds on Great South Bay, Long Island, were known to the Shinnecock Indians long before the first white man fired a fowling piece over the mud and reeds. Some locations for waterfowl blinds have been heavily used for hundreds of years.

The waterfowler should set up with his decoys where the prevailing wind blows from behind him toward his blocks. Waterfowl prefer to land coming into the wind. It's inconvenient and startling to have the birds burst upon the scene from the rear, and if your blind has no roof, the birds may see you and flare away. A crossing wind is better than a wind in your face. If possible, a duck blind should also be located where there are no high objects (such as a line of trees or a bluff just behind), since geese and diving ducks must make long runs across the water in order to take off. If there are high objects behind the blind, the birds are reluctant to come in and land on the water. They sense that they will be unable to get up enough speed in their run and low initial flight to clear the obstacles. This is not such a problem for surface-feeding ducks since they jump right into the air.

Points of land are often favored for blinds, since ducks and geese like to come in over water to land, if possible, and a blind on a point of land gives them three lines of approach, depending on the direction of the wind. A blind on an island or small sandbar is excellent too. If you are building a new blind, it's a good idea to watch the birds for a while before you begin to build. Set up near a feeding area wherever possible.

The simplest form of blind, often used by Indians and Eskimos, involves concealment of a duck boat or canoe, and is more of a camouflage technique. Crees and other northern Indians often use the same method to hunt moose in marshes and shallow lakes and sloughs.

In some areas, it is enough to run the canoe or duck boat up into the reeds or tall water grass and gently bend them over the boat. Camouflage cloth or a net with natural material woven into it is sometimes thrown over the boat and the hunters. Slits in the net provide a quick way to free gun or camera when you wish to shoot. If you are using firearms and the water is fairly deep, it sometimes pays to drive stakes at both sides and lash the boat to them so that the recoil of the shotgun or rifle will not put you overboard. This is important if you shoot to one side with a heavy shotgun from a canoe. Most duck boats are stable enough to absorb the recoil.

If a net or camouflage cloth is not used, the boat is often grassed up or iced up. Cover the boat with marsh grass or reeds, or if there is ice in the river or bay and snow on the ground, cover the decking and bottom planking with snow or ice. Sometimes a white sheet will simulate an ice floe or a patch of snow on a mudbank or small island.

The cove blind is either natural or artificial. If you can find a place where a small inlet or narrow cove allows the boat to go right in among shoreline brush or reeds, the concealment problem is solved. If not, it may be possible to dig out a tiny boat harbor. If the ground is marshy and unstable, some hunters cut many saplings into three-foot lengths and drive them into the surrounding marshy ground before starting the excavation. The stakes are driven only four to six inches apart, and most of them are placed in front of the blind where the birds or other game is expected to appear. Then the shovel work begins. The concealed entrance is dug at a right angle or sharp curve so that the boat cannot be seen from the water. The muck is thrown among the stakes until a high enough bank surrounds and conceals the boat harbor.

The stake blind is usually built in the spring or early summer, so that reeds, marsh grass, and other vegetation can grow on the excavated muck and in a short while hide boat harbor, boat, and hunters. Men who use this type of waterfowl blind often shoot from their seats in the boat, but if the walls of the blind are firm and high enough, a small platform can be built inside. If sufficient vegetation

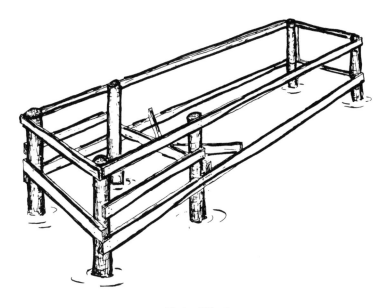

Stake Blind

does not spring up on the surrounding bank by the middle of summer, it's a good idea to transplant marsh grass or reeds from a different location. Some of these artificial coves are large enough to hold two or even three duck boats, kayaks, or canoes. Lashing the boats together provides a stable platform for shooting or the use of binoculars and camera.

Pit blinds are often used in open country where the vegetation isn't high. Indian hunters often dug pits when hunting plains game such as antelope, and modern hunters do the same where it proves impossible to stalk the animals. Pit blinds are also useful on sandbars, bare points, and mudbanks when hunting waterfowl. The birds do not expect a man or a predator to rise up out of flat, bare ground.

Big wooden boxes or barrels caulked or covered with waterproof fabric to keep water out are often sunk in marshy ground. A wood lid hinged at one side keeps out the rain when the blind is not in use, but it's a good idea to keep a boat pump or a bailer handy in a waterproof pit blind just in case it springs a leak. If the hinge pins are kept free by greasing them often, a wooden lid can be removed and concealed at a distance from the blind. A waterproof fabric cover does the job well enough if it can be lashed tightly to the rim of the sunken blind.

Foraging waterfowl often swim within range of pit blinds, especially if the hunter has a good decoy rig out. Flying birds are another matter. They may fly over and look down into the blind and flare when they see the hunter, but a camouflage net woven with vegetation or matching camouflage clothing is the answer. Keep your head down and do not show the whites of your eyes until you are ready to shoot or click the shutter. A line of transplanted vegetation on the edge of the pit blind makes this easy, but don't put in vegetation if there is none indigenous to the site.

There are many kinds of elaborate framework blinds. Most of them consist of a wood frame covered with chicken wire or netting with natural vegetation woven into the mesh. The chief problem with these blinds and big floating blinds is whether or not to cover them with a roof made of netting and vegetation, or even a more solid roof.

The eyesight of geese and ducks is almost unbelievable, and these birds are very sensitive to color. A single brightly colored cartridge case or sunlight glancing off a bright camera or gun part is enough to make them flare. A roof helps to prevent this since the birds cannot look down into the blind, but the roof does cause some inconvenience when shooting with camera or gun.

Some hunters solve this dilemma with a lightly built framework roof or netting covered with vegetation. Holes are left through which the birds can be seen, and the roof is thrown back when they come over. More often, the roof is merely elevated a bit and gun or camera is used from underneath it, shooting forward toward the decoys.

If you are hunting in heavily wooded country or flooded river bottoms, a roof is seldom needed. The birds fly in to decoys and calling, and they are within range overhead so quickly that you can do your shooting before they can flare away. In more open country, a roof is often a necessity, especially in areas where the wind is likely to veer all around the compass and bring birds in from behind the blind. It's a good idea to look at waterfowl blinds in the neighborhood before selecting a location and beginning to build. Experienced hunters in the area are usually adept at building the right kind of blind. Model yours after the local pattern.

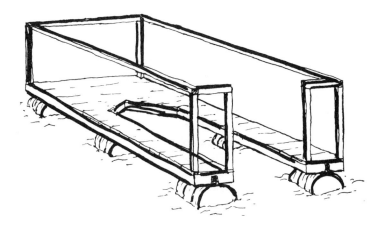

Floating Blind

Floating blinds with and without roofs or partial covering are merely large rafts covered with netting and vegetation. The walls may be formed of cut reeds placed upright between horizontal slats mounted on uprights. As a rule, boat floats or 55-gallon oil drums are used for flotation. These blinds are often anchored quite far offshore, and if this is done, enough brush or other vegetation must be used to make the entire floating battery look like a small island. In some cases, one side of the blind is hinged, and the center of the raft is cut away to accommodate the hunter's boat. The boat is taken into the blind, the gate is closed, and the gunner shoots from a seat in the boat through an opening in the top of the blind or stands on slats nailed across the boat harbor, high enough to clear his boat. All floating batteries should be securely anchored or they may drift away. Don't use new rope for anchor lines. Waterfowl can see bright new lines through clear water, and the unnatural straight lines of the anchor ropes can also spook them. Skillful hunters even use dull brown or green cords to anchor their decoys.

How Indians Used Animals as Cover

Many different kinds of portable blinds were used by Indians and early frontiersmen, and some of them are still useful today. Some of these portable blinds are a form of camouflage. For instance, there was the well-known "stalking horse." Geese, turkeys, and even plains game such as antelope don't seem to mind a horse or a steer that approaches fairly close. Indians and early white hunters often took advantage of this by walking up to game behind a domestic animal. The horse was encouraged to go on grazing as he angled obliquely toward the game, and the hunter tried to keep pace with the animal's legs in order to conceal himself while crouching down behind the horse's withers. This form of hunting was so effective that it is now specifically outlawed by federal statute for goose hunting and all other migratory waterfowl. Many a Canada honker, feeling secure when feeding out in the middle of an open field, was brought down easily with the stalking horse.

Indians often covered themselves with animal skins and moved right up on the game. Pronghorn antelope were hunted in this way, and some western Indians covered their heads with the heads and capes of deer. It would be foolhardy to do this nowadays, but the method could be used successfully by a photographer during the closed season.

Few land birds are hunted from blinds, though turkey hunters sometimes use small temporary hides made of leafy branches or reeds. The trouble with this method is that turkeys move about fast, especially when they are pushed by hunters. Building a blind is a gamble. The birds may never show up near it; so most turkey hunters rely on good camouflage clothing and calling.

Crow Blinds

Crows are just as clever as the wariest waterfowl, and their sensitivity to color and movement is even greater. A good blind for crows must match the surroundings well, and when the birds have been shot at a great deal, the concealed hunter must be a skilled caller. Crow blinds can often be placed on flyways between their night roosts and fields where the birds feed. Sometimes a pit blind with a fabric or netting roof is the right answer if there is little surrounding cover. Canvas or burlap cloth may be used for crow blinds if the right colors are painted on and the cloth hangs naturally from the branches or stakes used as supports. Good calling, silhouette decoys, and perhaps a stuffed owl to excite the hatred of the crows usually bring them in.

If a blind is built in the open, it must conceal the hunter on all sides. Crows often circle before coming in unless they are mobbing owl, hawk, or cat, and a three-sided or semicircular blind doesn't work well. If you build a crow blind in low vegetation, match its height. A blind that is higher than the brush is regarded with suspicion by most crows. This is especially true of blinds made of sheaves of grain or shocks of corn. A sheave or shock blind used to conceal a single hunter may be thicker than a real bound stack of grain, but if it is higher, crows will flare.

Elevated Blinds

Some tree blinds are complex and involve constructing a platform in a tree, or if a suitable crotch cannot be found, nailing the platform to the trunks of two or more trees growing close together. Elaborate concealment is not required because game seldom looks up, but the blind should be built of weathered logs or lumber. A deer appears to have good eyesight at a distance, and when the animal is far away from the blind, it may come within the angle of his vision. A deer underneath a blind is much less likely to see it or catch movement.

It's important to conceal the ladder or wooden steps used to climb up into an elevated blind. If you nail slats to a tree trunk as a ladder, make sure that you do it long before the season opens so that they weather well. Sometimes it is possible to pull a ladder up into the tree with you and lash it there. Check state and provincial regulations before building a blind or taking an elevated perch. Some jurisdictions forbid elevated blinds in trees because they are so effective.

When shooting from an elevated stand, most hunters have a tendency to shoot over the backs of the game with rifle or bow. Practice shooting at a steep downward angle before the season opens to overcome this handicap. This practice is most important for bowhunters because of the curved trajectory of their shafts.

The Indian Stalking Screen

Some northern Indians and Eskimos use a stalking screen to hunt seals and caribou, and this type of screen would be useful in some kinds of wildlife photography. It is shown in the accompanying drawing. It is a wooden framework covered with fabric—white for snow, camouflage cloth, or vegetation sewn to burlap. A cord tied to the two crossed sticks is used to carry it when stalking game, and a slit or two allows the hunter to see the quarry. The hunter is careful to move the screen toward the game only when the animal has its head down to feed or is looking away. It's most effective when the game is approached from rising ground. If the top of the screen is kept below the skyline, the screen blends into the slope.

Adapting Blinds to Local Conditions

A blind constructed to meet the exact conditions is often much more effective than a standard blind taken from any book, but it takes a little ingenuity to build one. Here's an example. On the big im-

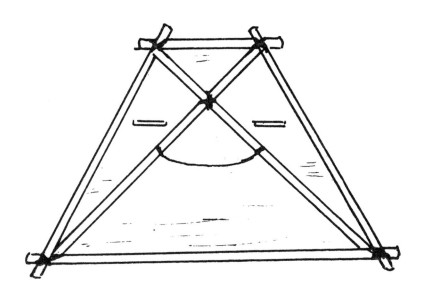

Indian Stalking Screen

poundments of the South, geese and ducks abound, but the only cover in shallow water and along the muddy beaches consists of the numerous stumps left after timber drowned when the dams were built. Freshwater vegetation has not sprung up; so the usual waterfowl blinds would not work well. In the fall, there is usually a considerable stretch of exposed mud dotted by big stumps; so some southern hunters dress up like stumps.

A roll of sheet metal is painted on the outside with drab paints to resemble a waterlogged stump, and a pivoting lid made of a wooden barrel end or a piece of sheet metal is mounted on a stake driven down inside the sheet-metal tube. The lid is painted too. The hunter sets out his decoys and erects his stump blind. When the birds fly in, the hunter spots them through the crack between the lid and the blind's sides, or pivots the lid aside and takes duck or goose.

7 /

Outwitting
Small Game

RABBITS, HARES, and squirrels provide good hunting throughout the United States. Probably more hunters learn their craft by going after these animals than any other, and this was true of the young Indian, who learned a great deal about deer and elk hunting by using his first bow on the elusive squirrel and the erratic rabbit and hare.

The cottontail rabbit is small, fourteen to sixteen inches long, and weighs no more than two or three pounds. The white puffy tail, distinguishing the cottontail from the larger hares, is clearly visible even at a distance when the animal is going away fast. Local variations of the cottontail include the New England variety, the desert cottontail, the swamp rabbit, and the marsh rabbit. The ranges of these animals often overlap. For the hunter, the animals are much the same and inhabit similar territories, except for the swamp rabbit and the marsh rabbit, both of which favor freshwater swales in the South.

In Europe, rabbits live by the thousands in large warrens and dig their own burrows. They dig so many holes in a confined area that they often undermine roads, railroad right-of-ways, and even airfields. In the United States, "rabbits" and hares do not live crowded together, and they rarely dig their own burrows. Instead, they establish forms—nests in depressions in the ground often lined

Cottontail Rabbit

with soft grasses and the fur of the doe. Sometimes, however, cottontails take refuge in burrows dug by other animals, the woodchuck in particular. If this happens when you are hunting, it's almost useless to try to dig the rabbit out since it will use the escape hole made by the chuck. Digging out rabbits or almost any form of game is illegal in most states.

In the United States and Canada, the term "hare" includes the arctic hare, the snowshoe hare (sometimes called the snowshoe rabbit), and the various jackrabbits of the West. Among the latter are the black-tailed jack, the white-sided jack, and the white-tailed jack. All species of hare are larger and heavier than the various forms of cottontail. The white-tailed jack may be as long as twenty-eight inches, and weigh as much as ten pounds. The meat of the jacks is stringy, tough, and almost without flavor. The Indians and most white men prefer the flesh of the cottontail. Arctic hares and the snowshoe rabbit (varying hare) are good eating.

In upper New York State and the area around the Great Lakes in the United States and Canada, the hunter may be confused when he brings down a big hare resembling the black-tailed jackrabbit but with no black on its rump. This is the European hare, long escaped from the hutches of early settlers and gone wild. Eastern Indians soon discovered that this hare is flavorful and big enough to be meaty.

HUNTING COTTONTAILS

Walking Them Up

Walking them up assures a well-filled bag if the hunter knows the terrain and where rabbits are likely to be found. After a slight snow, look for tracks to locate concentrations of them. Even when there is no snow, you can often locate the well-worn runways that the cottontail establishes in thick cover such as brier patches, thick clumps of berry bushes, and other dense vegetation. Overgrown pastures and fields near woods and other fringe areas are always a good bet.

Cottontails prefer thorny bushes or vines for cover because they can run below the thorns, though dogs, foxes, coyotes, and larger birds of prey find it difficult to negotiate that kind of cover. Some

Cottontail Rabbit Tracks

Woodland Indians wore full-length rawhide leggings that resembled the chaps worn by cowmen for this kind of hunting. Nowadays, cottontail hunters often wear heavy leather-faced trousers.

The cottontail has only two defenses against predators and hunters—concealment and a fast escape. The well-camouflaged cottontail can hide in a clump of dry grass or leaves which seems too small to conceal even a mouse. If you look for the large, dark eye, you may spot the rabbit.

Bolting the Cottontail

To bolt the cottontail from its hide, try the Indian trick of taking a few steps and then standing stock still for a minute or two. The rabbit may panic and break cover. If two or three hunters work together, walking a stretch of cover abreast, it's best for all of them to pause and wait at frequent intervals. Good hunters, who know how to walk and stop, can often get their limits out of a single abandoned pasture, while the man who insists on walking miles may pass through the same territory without getting a single shot.

Locating the Runways

In heavy cover, it may be possible to trail-watch for cottontails. Go through the cover slowly some time when you are not hunting or when the season is closed and look for the runways. The best place to stand is where two or more runways cross, and when you go out with your gun or bow, try to stay downwind. You'll often find tufts of rabbit hair caught on thorns and branches if the runway is used often. Sitting on a good runway early in the morning or late in the afternoon when cottontails are on the move will often put a few of them in the bag.

Hunting with Partners and Dogs

You'll get better results if you have a partner who walks the runways, getting a shot now and then himself, and putting rabbits on the move toward you. Take a stand just off the runway in a good patch of cover. A good beagle or basset hound is even better than a human trail-walker because the hound will often follow scent into the surrounding thorns and scare a rabbit out onto the runway. Two men with one dog make an excellent team. While one man sits, the other walks the dog about and releases it. Some hunters use packs of a dozen dogs on big hunts.

Indian hunters knew that the cottontail holes up in a chuck burrow or form when cold winds begin to blow. There he waits the weather out until it improves and the ice and snow melt off his food. If you follow the practice of the Indians by hunting shortly after a windstorm or cold weather ends, the rabbits will be foraging for meals they missed during the bad weather, and you'll have a better chance at them.

When started by a hound, the cottontail usually runs in circles, to hurry back to home territory, where he knows the runways and the thick thorn patches. Since that is the rabbit's best chance of evading the eager hound, the hunter often stays where the hound put the game up, though a partner or two may follow along in the hope of getting a shot ahead of the dogs.

A good beagle follows his rabbit by scent alone, and he works at it slowly; so it is not an all-out chase. Unlike a fox or a coyote, the cottontail doesn't line out ahead of hounds. Instead, he hops along for a while and takes a rest while the hound works on the scent trail behind him. A hunter on foot who uses a close-working dog that understands the game can keep up with the beagle. If the dog is the short-legged, slow-moving basset, it's easy. The dog was bred for slow hunting in Belgium and France. The dog often moves along only five or six feet in front of the hunter. If the hunter cannot keep up with the dog, the rabbit may circle back to the man who waited where it originally flushed.

Weapons and Ammunition

Modern hunters use shotguns when hunting the cottontail, and loads of No. 6 shot are best to put him down. A few skilled hunters use .22 rifles or handguns. The Indians used blunt arrows to knock them down, and modern bowhunters usually use blunts too. A broadhead destroys too much meat when it hits the small animal. Some hunters compromise by using field points. The man who goes out with bow and arrow after cottontails is taking on a tough challenge. In the thick cover the animals prefer, it's hard to get a shot at a sitting cottontail where the arrow will not be deflected from the target by the brush, and a running, dodging cottontail is a difficult target for the bowman.

The bowhunter's best chance to get his cottontail is to spot it while it is sitting in the open. That's difficult unless you have developed an ability to spot game that is as good as a fine Indian hunter's. A bowhunter can do well enough with a slow, close-working dog. The dog starts a rabbit and follows the scent with the bowhunter almost stepping on his dog's tail. The rabbit hops along and pauses for a rest. If the hunter's eye is sharp, if he's a good-enough marksman, and if the cover is open enough, he may get in a killing shot.

Trail-watching sometimes pays off for the bowhunter too. If the hunter is alone, sooner or later a cottontail will come along the runway.

Many rabbit hounds like to mouth the game after it is put down. The shotgunner has no objection because the shot in the rabbit cannot harm the dog, and mouthing the game keeps the hounds interested in the chase. If the bowhunter is using any form of pointed arrow instead of blunts, however, the dog's mouth may be cut or pierced by the head. If you bowhunt with dogs, you risk injury to valuable animals by using pointed arrows, but some game cannot be killed without sharp points or edges. Call the dog off or pull it off the game as soon as you can. It's difficult to break a hound of the habit of mouthing the game once he has learned to enjoy it.

Cottontail Drives

In some southern states, country people still employ an old Indian hunting method. A big drive for cottontails is organized, in which every farm boy participates, and the good rabbit cover is soon surrounded. The rabbits are driven out into the open. Each man carries a rabbit stick—a short length of hardwood, perhaps with a railroad nut wired to its end to add extra throwing weight. When a rabbit gets up or comes by, a well-aimed stick whirling end-over-end kills it just as quickly as a blunt-headed arrow, and these big drives are safe since the thrown stick seldom injures a man seriously.

In the West, farmers sometimes organize big drives to exterminate jackrabbits that are damaging crops, but in those drives shotguns are often used.

JACKRABBITS

Indian Horseback Hunts

A somewhat similar method of hunting jackrabbits was employed by some western tribes, and the Navajos still use it at times. It is one of the most dangerous forms of hunting in North America. Several tribes hunted jackrabbits on horseback. Their only weapons were hardwood sticks about two feet long. Sometimes they could hit the jack by leaning down from the horse, but the stick was thrown too. If the hunter missed, he leaned down from his mount to recover his stick, often while the horse was still moving fast. This form of rabbit hunting resembles polo, but it is much more hazardous. A horse may step into a hole, break a leg, and throw the rider.

A line of mounted hunters moved across the flat until the jack got up; then there was bedlam. The Indians' ponies could run a jack down, and the rabbit often took refuge by turning and running in among the hoofs of the horses. Collisions, falls, broken bones, and hell-for-leather riding provided thrills.

The reward for a kill was honor. Few jacks were killed, but the man who brought one down, and above all, the man who rode hard and showed no fear of injury or death, won tribal acclaim. That was excellent practice for buffalo hunters who used lance or bow and arrow from horseback.

Hunting with Long-Range Rifle

The jackrabbit nowadays is a target for the long-range rifleman out to test his skill with distant targets in preparation for the big-game season. He takes his place on a rise of ground with binoculars and scoped rifle or he tries to find jacks by moving slowly through the mesquite and cactus. A big western jack moves along at an astonishing pace when he wants to, and if you can bring him down with a big-game rifle, elk, mule deer, or antelope will present few problems. Most western states have no closed season on jackrabbits, and there is no bag limit because the animals are so destructive to crops. Western farmers often use poison to eliminate large colonies of the pests. For the long-range rifleman, however, the big western jacks provide the kind of training needed later for open-country mule deer and pronghorn antelope.

Hunting with Shotgun

Shotgunners find jacks difficult to walk up in open country, though they sometimes do get a shot or two. It's more like wingshooting than rabbit hunting. Jacks often cover ten to eighteen feet in their leaps, and a leap may be as much as six feet high. You hope that a jack will jump high above the scrub. Swing the gun fast, and fire rapidly as the animal reaches maximum height. That type of shooting is good training for hunting ruffed grouse and quail.

Stillhunting for jacks with a bow is a demanding sport. The jack is exceptionally wary, and the hunter needs fine footwork and excellent vision.

The rifleman gets most of his shots early in the morning and late in the afternoon when jacks are ranging wide to forage; the bowhunter does best during the hotter portion of the day when the animals are lying up in the shade under mesquite scrub and other vegetation. Walk stealthily into the wind, pausing after every ten or twelve steps to search the cooler hollows under bushes for a jack. If possible, take your shot at the resting animal before he can jump. If you can get a jack that way, you're an excellent stillhunter. If you don't succeed and the jack escapes, you'll still get fine practice for wingshooting with a bow—a form of archery that few hunters master.

THE NORTHERN HARES

The varying hare (snowshoe rabbit) and the arctic hare of the Northland are the staple food of the predators—lynx, hawk, owl, fox, wolf—and they provide much food for northern Indians and Eskimos.

The arctic hare is seldom hunted by white men because its range is in the very far north—Newfoundland, Labrador, northern Quebec, the Arctic coast into Alaska. White men who hunt in that territory are usually nonresidents hunting for big game. White resident hunters, Indians, and Eskimos, however, hunt the hare eagerly in much the same way that the varying hare is hunted a little farther south.

Spotting in Snow

Both of these northern hares vary in color. The animals are dark in summer but in winter turn white except for the tips of the ears, which remain black. The large, dark eye can be seen at a distance. On the white snow, the stillhunter looks for the white hares in vain unless he concentrates on seeing the isolated tips of the ears and the eye. You will see these spots in threes as a rule, since hares see best from the side and turn the sides of their heads toward the approaching predator or hunter. The combination looks like a period with two exclamation-point tops. If you see these motionless, it's time to shoot, and in the circumstances, it's easy to put a bullet through the animal's head, or if you are a good bowman, an arrow through the body.

When Color Change Makes the Hares Conspicuous

As northern Indians and Eskimos know, there are times when it is much easier to spot the quarry. These two large hares turn white as cold weather advances, but the color change often takes place before the first snowfall if the weather remains clear and rather warm. If the first snows are late, the hare finds himself with a white coat on dull brown pine needles or leaves, among the evergreens, or on bare, dark stones. The opposite happens too, the animal retaining his dark fur, or patches of it, when there is a smooth white fall of snow on the ground. That's the time when the Indian gets many hares. The archer finds it easier to get close to the animal because it is so easy to spot. If one gets away, it's easy to spot another that may stay put. Since they are large and rather heavy, it's best to hunt hares with broadheads unless your bow is powerful enough to kill with blunts.

The Indian Way to Freeze Hares

An Alaskan Indian guide once demonstrated an odd way to hunt hares. Snow had fallen, but the big hares were still dark. The guide and his client were going through low scrub on foot and saw several hares hopping slowly away from them. The animals showed some white but looked mostly grayish black against the snow. The guide suddenly let out a series of yells that sounded like a cross between an eagle's screaming and the weird yowls of a bobcat. Yelling as he went, he made for the nearest hare. When his partner came up, the Indian was bending over the hare with a .22 single-shot pistol in his hand. He shot the hare through the head as it cowered behind a log. The guide revealed that he often took the hares that way and that many of his people did the same. Even a pistol isn't necessary. The hare can be killed with a stick or a blow from the edge of the hand on the back of the neck.

Evidently, the weird screaming sounds like the fiercest predator in the woods to the timid hare, and the animal suddenly becomes so terrified that it simply cannot run away. It doesn't always work, though.

Hunting with Hounds

The varying hare (snowshoe rabbit) is often hunted with dogs in the southern part of its range, but many hunters find that the beagle is not up to the job. The snowshoe rabbit has large, splayed feet and runs on snow where a beagle flounders. A larger hound is best. The snowshoe rabbit runs bigger circles than the cottontail, and runs faster. If you plan to hunt snowshoe rabbits, you might look around for a few big crossbred hounds. Keep in mind, though, that if you permit them to hunt for any kind of rabbit or hare, they become useless for any other form of hunting. If a hound runs rabbits, he'll desert a bobcat or coyote track the first time he comes across rabbit scent.

A few sportsmen like to run varying hares ahead of hounds in open country and shoot them with auto-loading .22 rifles. The hounds run the hare in a circle, and as it comes past the hunter, the rifleman swings through, gets a bit ahead with his sights, and pulls the trigger. If he does not get a hit, he keeps ahead, and shoots again with the semi-automatic.

How Bowhunters Can Get Sitting Shots

Strangely enough, the snowshoe hare is a possible target for the bowhunter, as the Indians knew. On still, clear, cold days when there is a bright sun, the animal lazes about, enjoying the weather. Then you can get a sitting shot. A running shot with a bow is difficult, though the northern hares are not nearly so airborne as the western jacks.

SQUIRRELS

There are five kinds of tree squirrels in the United States, and the range of some of them extends into Canada.

The most common is the familiar gray squirrel of the East, which becomes almost tame where hunting is not permitted. It can be a nuisance as well. In the wild, the gray squirrel is a clever, wary game animal. These animals weigh about one pound.

Gray Squirrel

Many squirrel hunters have never seen a fox squirrel because they have grown scarce in some areas, although the overall range of the fox squirrel is about the same as that of the gray. These animals have much more red in their fur and are sometimes called big red squirrels or red-tailed squirrels. They weigh from about 2¼ to 2¾ pounds. The fox squirrel is so large that he looks as big as a marten to the man who is used to hunting grays. The fox squirrel is much clumsier in trees than the gray or any other tree squirrel, and that may be the reason why this animal is almost extinct in some parts of his range. A hunter usually has little difficulty in hitting a fox squirrel, and predators find it an easy prey.

The tiny red squirrel is edible too, but is so small that few men hunt him. It is only about ten inches long and the tail makes up four to six inches of this length. The average weight is less than half a pound.

How Indians Silenced the Red Squirrel

The reddish-pelted animal, often called chickaree, is a woods sentinel. The red squirrel seems unafraid of hunters, perhaps because he is seldom hunted, and scolds intruders noisily. Often a deer stalk is spoiled by a nervous chickaree scolding the silent stillhunter, who should try to get away from red as quickly as possible. Even then, red may follow, scolding the hunter and alerting every deer for hundreds of yards. Indian hunters often avoided his scolding by moving silently and staying away from nut trees and den trees where he was likely to be found or by screaming like a hunting hawk. This scares a chickaree and makes him freeze until the hunter passes by. The hawk scream must be a perfect imitation in order to avoid frightening off the deer or other game you are hunting.

The red squirrel is regarded as vermin in many states and no limit or closed season is imposed, though a few states do classify him as a game animal. He is destructive and eats nestlings and eggs. Reds also seem to be able to kill off the larger gray squirrel in certain areas and take over that more valuable animal's range. They do this by raiding the nests of gray squirrels and killing the kits to eat, but sometimes a tiny red squirrel pursues the larger gray adult and bites at his rear. Sometimes the red manages to do an effective castration job.

Hunting the red squirrel is good conservation. Where there is no limit, a dozen or more in the stew pot make an excellent meal. Woodland Indians often used them for food when other game was scarce.

There is a California gray squirrel, and there are two forms of tassel-eared squirrels that inhabit the area along the Colorado River, but few westerners hunt squirrels for food. The few who do are almost always from back East. Western hunters are missing a good bet when they disdain tree squirrels as game.

Most tree squirrels are subject to melanism, and albinos are to be found. In some areas, you may run across glossy-black gray squirrels. These are melanistic, though some southern hunters insist that they are a separate species.

Squirrels' Favorite Foods

All tree squirrels eat nuts, fruits, berries, seeds, some soft twigs and bark, a few kinds of fungus, and some farm crops, especially corn. The primary food of the fox squirrel and the gray is nuts, and you'll almost always find these animals among oaks, beech trees, hickories, and other nut trees. Since the Indians gathered many different kinds of nuts for their own food, an Indian squirrel hunter had an advantage over most modern urban hunters. While gathering nuts, he kept an eye open for a flaunting tail. If you want to hunt squirrels successfully, one good way to prepare yourself is to study trees so that you can recognize nut-bearers at a distance. When you can pick out a black walnut among the other trees in a grove, you'll probably find squirrels in it if it is nut-bearing at the time.

Best Guns and Ammunition

In settled areas, most modern hunters use shotgun shells loaded with No. 6 shot to hunt squirrels. The shot does not carry far, and even if it does fall almost straight down on a man, it does little or no harm. The .22 rifle is the second most popular weapon, though it should be remembered that the .22 Long Rifle cartridge carries at least a mile at high elevation, and therefore accidents are possible. Even a shot at a squirrel on the ground is dangerous since the low-velocity .22 bullet seldom shatters on impact with a rock or other hard surface, and a ricocheting bullet may carry a long distance. Hunting squirrels with a .22 is an interesting sport. If you manage to hit the squirrel in the head with your bullet, you'll avoid spoiling the meat of the body or hind legs, but it takes a good rifleman to do it. Most of them use a low-power scope. Hunting bushytails with a .22 handgun improves marksmanship and fills the pot.

Best Arrows and Fletching

Indian bowmen used blunt arrows and flu-flu fletching on squirrels because they did not wish to spoil the meat and because that type of arrow does not fly far; so it is not lost so often in case of a miss. Broadheads spoil a lot of meat, and a falling broadhead arrow that misses a squirrel can kill or injure a man when it drops to earth. If you shoot pointed arrows into trees at squirrels, many of them will lodge in trunk or limbs. Unless you climb trees to recover them, you can lose a lot of them in one day.

"Barking"

Frontiersmen often used muzzleloading rifles to "bark" squirrels. Grays and fox squirrels often freeze when they see a hunter. The muzzleloading rifle was aimed to hit branch or trunk right under the squirrel's chest. When the round ball hit, it almost always hit the branch beside the squirrel and the concussion killed or stunned the animal, leaving the skin and body undamaged.

Squirrels can bite deeply enough to make a nasty wound. If you stun or wound a squirrel, don't pick it up too soon. The Indians often finished off squirrels by pressing a foot firmly on the animal's shoulders below the neck so that the squirrel could not bite the moccasined foot. The pressure stopped the heart and lungs. This method works well with other small game.

Stillhunting

Stillhunting for squirrels is primarily a matter of recognizing good country in which to hunt them and stalking in silence. Some stillhunters use squirrel calls to imitate the contented sounds that the animals make when they have found abundant food. Indian hunters often tapped and rubbed two round, smooth pebbles together to imitate a squirrel chewing on a nut shell to get at the meat inside. Most of the time, those two sounds will bring squirrels to the feast through the treetops. Since the squirrels usually travel fairly high in the

Gray Squirrel Tracks

treetops, the hunter seldom has to worry about his scent reaching the animals. A good stillhunter moves silently through the woods, but should pause often to conceal himself and call. Sometimes the squirrels will not come but they will answer, and then the hunter stalks them.

Hunting in Pairs

The gray squirrel is an expert at keeping a tree trunk between himself and the hunter. If you're on one side of the tree, the squirrel almost always seems to be on the opposite side. He often climbs the tree on that side until he reaches the crown and then jumps to another tree without being seen. Indians often hunted squirrels in pairs, and modern hunters often do the same. When two hunters approach a nut tree and a squirrel whisks around to the other side, one man remains where he is, weapon ready, and the other quickly moves around the tree. One or the other will usually get a shot. If there is a third man in the party, he backs off a few yards so that he can see the topmost branches. Often he is able to pick off the squirrel if it is out of sight of the two other men.

Indian Ruses for Fooling Squirrels

If you're hunting alone, it sometimes helps to prop up your coat and perhaps your hat on a bush near the tree. When you go around the trunk, the squirrel will usually circle around too. When he sees your coat and hat, he may become alarmed and freeze for an instant, so that you may get a shot.

Some Indian hunters carried a long fiber cord or thong. When the squirrel dodged around the trunk, the Indian hitched the line to a sapling or bush before he went around the trunk. When the squirrel came around to his original position, the Indian pulled on the line to shake the bush or sapling violently. This often held the squirrel's attention so that the hunter could fire. Modern squirrel hunters who use this trick often tie a short stick to the end of the line. It's quicker to hitch the stick behind a low fork in a bush than it is to tie the line.

Sitting for Squirrels

Some hunters find it pays off to sit for squirrels. Take up a favorable position near or in a grove of hardwoods and remain quiet. If you can conceal yourself, so much the better. Some Indians lie prone on the ground on their backs and shoot from that position, and many shot-gunners and riflemen do the same. Putting leaves over yourself to break up your outline helps, and some men carry a camouflage ground cloth that they throw over themselves, but that's dangerous in heavily hunted squirrel groves.

If you know of a den tree, try sitting for squirrels there. As a rule, a den tree has large hollows where branches have broken off and the stub has rotted out, or the trunk may be hollow. Some hunters sit near a den tree and then use their calls to make the alarmed sounds that squirrels make when they spot a predator or a hunter. That often brings the squirrels running to the shelter of the den tree, and the hunter may be able to take as many as three or four of them as they come.

Squirrels sometimes ignore the discharge of a rifle or a shotgun. After a shot, remain still, and the animals will begin to move again in fifteen minutes or so. If you are sitting for squirrels, it's wise to let cleanly killed animals lie until you are finished hunting in that area. Mark where they fall by noting bushes, branches, or stones near the animal and wait until you are finished before picking up the kill. The less you move, the better.

Squirrel hunters sometimes concentrate so much on watching tree trunks and high branches that they miss squirrels on the ground. If berries and fruits are available on low bushes or have fallen to the ground, or if the nuts are falling, you may find squirrels almost under-foot if you walk quietly enough.

Some squirrel hunters have the unsportsmanlike habit of firing a charge of shot into every squirrel nest they see in hopes of knocking a squirrel out of them. These leafy breeding nests are almost always empty by the time the hunting season starts.

Best Hunting Weather

On windy, cold days or when rain or snow is falling, squirrels remain at home and wait the weather out; so it's wiser to hunt on calm, rather warm days, and the best time is early in the morning or late in the afternoon. Squirrel hunting, as the Indians knew, is usually good just after a cold snap or a storm has ended because the denned-up animals come out to make up for lost time in their feeding.

If you hunt during bad weather, the middle of the day is sometimes productive. The squirrel stays at home until hunger drives him to feed, and that's usually later in the day than usual. If the weather is bad during the forenoon, but improves later in the day, that's the time to be out with gun or bow.

Good Squirrel Dogs

Some mongrel Indian dogs were good squirrel hunters, and many a crossbred farm dog does as well. The small mongrel, preferably one with just a little terrier or hound blood in him, does better at squirrel hunting than most purebred dogs. A good squirrel dog works close to the hunter so that the man will be ready when a squirrel shows. Often, the dog finds a squirrel by sight or scent on the ground and trees the animal. The sight of a dog on the ground rarely alarms a squirrel in a tree. But the dog attracts the squirrel's attention, and the hunter often finds it easy to drop the animal.

Good squirrel dogs are capable of following a fleeing squirrel merely by listening for scratches on the bark and the whoosh of the branches as the squirrel jumps from tree to tree. Good squirrel dogs seem to understand that it is not useful to put a squirrel up a tree or spot one on a branch if the hunter is not nearby.

OPOSSUMS

The opossum is the only pouched animal native to North America. The name, of Algonquin origin, describes an animal that carries its young in a pouch.

The opossum is covered with coarse, long, whitish outer hairs that conceal a soft underfur of darker color. The long, white face and mouth, long, pink nose, and hairless, ratlike tail give the opossum an ugly appearance. The "possum," as it is usually called, lives in every southern state east of the Mississippi, and though not common elsewhere, its range extends as far west as Iowa and Texas and into New York and southern New England. Quite a number of them were brought into California for private menageries. Several escaped, and now the animal is found in much of that state. The possum is one of

Opossum

the few animals in North America that is constantly expanding its range into new areas where it was never found before.

The possum survives as a species in spite of predators, dogs, and hunters because of its rapid, prolific reproduction.

Hunting with Dogs

Modern hunters take possums with dogs at night since the animal is almost entirely nocturnal, but early in the morning and late in the evening, they are sometimes seen in favored feeding grounds where they eat small birds, very small mammals, eggs, carrion, and some green plants.

Hunting possums with a dog is largely a matter of being on the spot when the dog barks "treed." Since the possum isn't active, he is often found on a low branch or in a bush; so it's easy to shake him out or climb up and throw him down. Then he's usually dispatched

Opossum Tracks

by the dogs or the hunter wielding a club. It's a leisurely sport, but in the rural South, many men enjoy an evening out with a dog or two.

The possum is so slow-moving and stupid that a man can often catch him without a dog or weapon, and the Indians did so on moonlit nights. The Indians also dug them out of their dens. For the southern tribesman, the possum occupied the same position as the porcupine. Since it's so easy to catch, the Indian found that the possum came in handy during emergencies when other food was scarce.

Early settlers learned to depend on the possum for food, and they often kept one or two that they had captured alive in a pen and fed them fresh vegetables and table scraps until the rather ill-tasting oil in their body fat thinned out.

When Opossums Turn Dangerous

The ability of the possum to play dead when caught by dogs, predators, or hunters is probably a function of this stupid animal's low-geared nervous system. The possum is overwhelmed by excitement and faints. If he survives, he revives and goes about his business. When a "dead" possum regains consciousness, he can give a very nasty bite.

PORCUPINES

These big, blundering rodents with their many quills grow to nearly a yard in length and may weigh over forty pounds. The barbed quills—

Porcupine

about 32,000 of them—give an adult porcupine the look of a black, elongated pincushion with white streaks. Porcupines like to sit in the high branches of a tree and sway back and forth in the wind. They are so large that it's quite possible to mistake one high in a tree for a bear cub.

To defend himself, porky pokes his unarmed face into shelter such as the space under a log or between ground and a boulder and lashes out with his quill-armed tail. If he's unusually aggressive, he'll "charge" suddenly backwards toward the enemy, but will likely lumber back to his improvised shelter.

The fisher (pekan), a big tree-climbing weasel, is about the only woods animal that manages to dine regularly on porcupines. The lightning-fast fisher turns the porcupine over onto his back and bites at the unprotected underside. Coyotes can do it too. One coyote engages porky's attention, and the other rushes in from the side and flips him over; then one or both may get in a killing bite.

The quills are hollow and enable the porcupine to float with ease, but he spends most of his time aloft eating tree bark and tender twigs, which makes him hated by tree farmers and timber companies. The porcupine will often work his way right around a trunk, eating bark as he goes. That girdles the tree and kills it. He also likes to eat canoe paddles, axes, and tool handles for the salty sweat on them.

The laws in some places prohibit the killing of porcupines except by a man who is lost in the woods and starving. The porcupine is so slow that a man can easily kill one with a club. If the bark and twig supply holds up, a porcupine will stay in a small clump of trees for an entire year, and he may stay in one small area for his entire life. If Indians saw a porcupine and had no immediate need for meat, they would note its location. When other game grew scarce, they often had several porcupines pinpointed and could kill them as needed. Since the porcupine does not hibernate, he is accessible all year round.

Porky lives in a stub hole in a tree, a cleft in the rocks, a cave, a hollow under tree roots or boulders—any shelter that doesn't require too much work to make it comfortable. Indian squaws often dug or rooted him out for the sake of his quills. The quills were used in the handsome decorative work on the buckskin garments of Woodland and other Indians. The quills take dye readily, and the squaws dyed them in many colors. Then they were cut into varied lengths and sewn onto garments in decorative patterns.

Porcupine Tracks

How Indians Pulled Porcupines from Their Dens

At times, squaws dug porky out, but usually it was enough to pull him out of his den with a stick. The squaw took a supple length of sapling about an inch thick and split one end of it to form four or more long, flexible "fingers." The porcupine stick was shoved into the den until contact was made, and then the stick was pushed and twisted until the ends caught in the animal's quills. The porcupine was then dragged out of the hole and killed with a club. If you try the same procedure, be sure about the identity of the animal in the hole. It may be a skunk. Tracks and sign near the den will usually identify the animal inside.

How to Extract Quills

A dog or a man pierced by quills may die because the barbed quills work their way into the flesh and may ultimately penetrate a vital organ. Get to a veterinarian or a doctor as quickly as you can, but if that is impossible, you must pull the quills out yourself with pliers. A dog should be firmly tied with a stick lashed between his jaws so that he cannot bite before you undertake the painful task. Snip the ends of the hollow quills off so that they deflate slightly and can be yanked out more easily. A good disinfectant should be used afterward since porky picks up a lot of dirt on his barbed quills.

WOODCHUCKS

The common chuck that burrows under boulders and stumps in almost every pasture in the eastern states and southern Canada is a surprisingly big and bold animal. A large adult weighs ten pounds or a little more, and he is well armed with strong rodent teeth and earth-moving claws.

The woodchuck feeds early and late on tender green vegetation including timothy, hay, alfalfa, and garden crops. His burrows are a constant hazard to horses and cattle.

Where Chucks Dig Their Burrows

The woodchuck's burrow is usually dug on rather high, dry ground,

Woodchuck Tracks

and it must be close to green ground vegetation, for the chuck does not climb trees and does not range far from home to feed.

Indian youngsters used to stalk woodchucks to demonstrate their stalking skill and courage. While the chuck was feeding outside his burrow, the would-be brave tried to place himself between the chuck and the entrance to the hole and then kill him with club or bow. The chuck is a brave animal, and the Indian youngster often found it difficult to stand up to the animal's angry growls and menacing jaws and meet its headlong charge.

Bowhunters often try this trick today, and find that the chuck hasn't changed. He is still one of the few animals in North America that will charge boy, man, or dog and bite when he attacks.

The Crees, Ojibways, and Algonquins all hunted the chuck for practice in stalking and shooting and for food when other game was scarce. A young chuck, carefully cleaned and cooked, is a tasty dish, and some modern hunters eat them. Today, the chuck is a valued animal in many areas because he provides a living target for long-range riflemen who go after him with the latest in flat-shooting

Woodchuck

firearms equipped with rifle scopes. Almost everywhere, farmers welcome the chuck hunter because he thins out these crop-eating rodents and helps to cut down on the number of dangerous chuck holes in the pastures.

The Right Ranges for Archers and Riflemen

The bowhunter who goes after chucks is taking on a tough challenge. The rifleman shoots from 100 yards or more for the sake of long-range practice, and will often hold his fire at short range. The bowhunter must get within fifteen or twenty yards of the small, wary target, and that's difficult in areas where the chucks have become hunter-shy. A chuck vanishes into long grass or down a hole so fast that he seems to disappear into thin air, but if you remain quiet, he often pops up again and sits up on his haunches to peer around. Walking heavily sends vibrations through the ground and warns the chuck to stay below.

The chuck remains in his burrow all winter and emerges in February or March. He goes below ground again with the first frost. Chucks seldom come above ground during bad weather.

In almost every state, the chuck is regarded as vermin by farmers and cattlemen, and he is a legal target whenever he can be found above ground. But in some areas where he is heavily hunted, sportsmen voluntarily refrain from killing young (small) chucks and nursing females with young following them. Thinning them out a bit helps the farmer; killing too many young ones and nursing females may cut down on the sport.

BADGERS

The North American badger is a well-armed, dangerous animal. He fears no animal except the wolf, the wolverine, and the bear. A pack of dogs that attacks a badger is in for a very rough time.

The badger is less than three feet long and weighs only about twenty pounds. He has short, thick legs and a flat body so that he hugs the ground and is difficult to spot even on the open, flat prairies where he is most often found. The forelegs are armed with long, sharp claws, and his teeth are formidable. He is a buffy-gray color with

Badger

white patches on face and the underside of the ears. The pelage is rough and coarse. He is the only animal in North America that has a narrow head and a single narrow white stripe down the back.

The badger lives at the end of a shallow burrow in a grassy nest. His food consists of small rodents such as prairie dogs that he digs out of the ground, small birds, eggs, and small snakes. Formerly, the badger was trapped and hunted for his bristly hair which was used to make shaving brushes.

How Indians Killed Badgers with Their Feet

Indian hunters stalked the badger and often tried to intercept him some distance from his burrow so that he could be killed with an arrow or a club. In order to demonstrate courage and agility, young Indians killed the badger in a way not recommended to modern hunt-

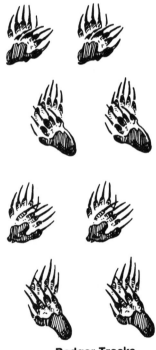

Badger Tracks

ers. After cutting off a badger from his burrow, the hunter ran swiftly until he was alongside or just behind the animal. Then he jumped high and landed hard on the badger's back with both feet. If the young hunter was quick and lucky, he killed the animal instantly by breaking its backbone. A hunter who failed in his leap was usually badly mauled by the animal's sharp teeth and claws. In a fight, the badger rolls onto his back with the swiftness of a wildcat and uses all his claws and teeth at the same time in self-defense.

Avoiding Injury from Wounded Badgers

If you wound a badger, never reach into his burrow to pull him out. Any number of inexperienced hunters and trappers died of starvation when they tried it. The wounded badger sinks his teeth into the man's forearm, retreats a little farther into the tunnel, and then sinks the long front claws into the earth. Once he is anchored in this position, he cannot be moved, and hunter and badger often die together.

OTHER SMALL GAME

On occasion, the Indians hunted several other small animals with bow and arrow or firearms. Muskrats and beaver were sometimes hunted, and the Indian trapper would do almost anything to rid himself of a raiding wolverine. Most often, though, the beaver, muskrat, wolverine, lynx, mink, marten, sable, river otter, the various weasels, and other small fur-bearers were and still are taken with traps and snares rather than firearms. The Aleuts of Alaska did hunt the sea otter from kayaks with harpoons, and after the Russian fur traders arrived, they sometimes used firearms too. The sea-otter trade led to the exploration of Alaska and Russian colonization there. It is interesting to know that the pursuit of this valuable fur-bearer by Indian hunters working for the Russians led to the early exploration of the western coast just as the lust for beaver pelts led to the exploration of much of the American and Canadian West.

8 /

Indian Tricks
For Taking Predators

SINCE 1946, VARMINT CALLING has grown enormously in popularity, and many people are rediscovering the ancient Indian art, which the tribesman used mostly to harvest furs. Wildlife photographers and nature observers too have taken up calling because it is often easier to call a predator to the camera or blind than it is to stalk him.

The typical varmint call imitates the unforgettable sound of a dying rabbit. Some calls imitate the squeals of a dying rat or the shrill notes of injured birds. The sound made by almost any small animal or bird in trouble works well. Foxes, coyotes, raccoons,* bobcats, the lynx, and wolves all respond to good calling, as do the various owls, hawks, magpies, and crows. Even the bald eagle and the golden eagle will come to this type of calling when you conceal yourself well, and it's a good way to get closeup photographs.

Expert callers disagree on how best to use varmint calls. Some of them call for several minutes at a time without interruption; others call for only a few seconds, stop for a few moments, and then repeat. Both methods are effective, but for the beginner, it's best to call sparingly. If you make only a few short calls with long pauses between them, it's less likely that you will make false sounds and frighten the quarry. Bobcats respond slowly to calls and approach with great caution. Foxes and coyotes come within about ten minutes unless they have been hunted this way before and have grown shy. If you call intermittently for about half an hour and nothing comes in, it may be best to move on.

THE SECRETS OF
SUCCESSFUL VARMINT CALLING

One secret of successful predator calling is to call with urgency, trying to get the sound of impending, agonized death into the sound. Unless driven by starvation, predators hunt when it's easiest; so varmint calling works best just after dawn and just before sunset when small animals and birds are feeding.

Try to locate game before setting up to call. Look for tracks, fox holes, the badger's den, farm damage done by coons, and the feathers or patches of torn fur and hide left by predators after they have dined.

Try to locate good downwind cover. If you believe that the area will produce predators from time to time, build a blind or even two or three so that you can switch around to accommodate changes in the wind or thermal currents. Sometimes it's enough to wear camouflage without using a blind, provided you take advantage of cover, keep low, and remain still and silent. There's no better nose afield than that of a fox or coyote, and if you attempt to call one in from downwind, you'll get no result.

Where predators are not hunted very much, they usually respond to a call by coming straight in, but where there is heavy hunting, the predator may be very shy. Bobcats have an astonishing ability to hunt and stalk silent and unseen. The camouflaged varmint hunter usually does not see the bobcat approach. One moment there is nothing; the next, the bobcat is glaring right at the caller. That's the moment for a quick shot or fast camera work. It's hard to fool a bobcat by moving weapon or camera slowly, and that's one reason why a good picture of a stalking bobcat is a rare photographic trophy. The Indians sometimes put out bait for coyotes and bobcats. Any carcass will do, but a fresh rabbit, guts ripped open to increase the scent, is among the best. If you want a bobcat photograph, put the bait upwind from your blind and focus a tripoded camera on it. Call until the cat comes in and starts to feed. Then click off. It works with a rifle too. Usually you can set up with the gun in a forked stick. Aim precisely and squeeze the trigger when the quarry is in the sights at the bait.

Often foxes, coyotes, and wolves circle before coming to the place where they think an injured animal or bird is struggling. If the animal circles the caller, it will cross the man's downwind scent. For that reason, many varmint hunters follow the Indian practice of locating at the foot of a cliff or bluff where the predator cannot circle behind and get downwind of the caller. If the wind permits, calling with a fast stream or a river to the rear works well too since most predators are reluctant to enter fast-flowing water. If you work with a partner, one man can call while the other waits downwind for the circling animal.

If you call a great deal in the late evening or at night (where legal), you'll call up a domestic cat gone wild. They are notorious destroyers of songbirds and small game. In most states, the conservation laws permit the hunter to kill the cat, and many official statements of conservation policy request the hunter to do so.

THE PREDATOR'S PLACE
IN THE ECOLOGICAL BALANCE

The word "varmint" was originally an American corruption of "vermin," meaning any destructive or troublesome bird or animal, particularly those that destroyed crops or domestic animals. The word "vermin" often includes mice, rats, some fur-bearers such as weasels, and pests such as crows, grackles, and starlings.

Today, the word "varmint" has a specialized meaning among hunters and is used to designate predators such as foxes, coyotes, bobcats, and wolves. No hunter would think of calling a mouse or a rat a varmint. The larger predators have gained status, and in many states they receive some legal protection. Formerly, there was no closed season on bobcats because they were classified as harmful animals, and some states paid bounties to hunters who killed them. Now many states have closed seasons on bobcats. Moves are now being made to class the timber wolf a game animal and set a closed season and a limit. The value of the predators is more widely understood, and people are beginning to realize that the predator has an important place in nature and is valuable to man. The predators kill off crippled and diseased game animals and fur-bearers and help curb the spread of disease. They also control the total population of many animals and prevent overgrazing and overbrowsing.

Even the coyote is getting some recognition for the good he does. In some western states, the coyote was almost poisoned out of existence because the animal sometimes killed domestic stock, especially lambs. Some of these areas then underwent a plague of field mice and other small rodents. Grain and pasture-grass seed was eaten so voraciously that some districts were turned into desert. In some of these places, stockmen who formerly shouted for government poisoners to destroy coyotes now appreciate the value of the animals. It's better to lose a few lambs than to have all your grazing land stripped so that sheep and beef cattle cannot exist on it.

It often turns out that the best means of predator control is the hunter. He keeps the animals thinned out, but cannot destroy all the predators, and that seems best for the landowner too. If predators become a problem, the rancher can use the varmint hunter as a control device by inviting a few responsible hunters onto enclosed private land to thin out the excess animals or any that prove to be the most destructive.

The primitive Indian did not have the white man's problem. His secret is that he lived with nature and seldom upset the relationship of one animal to another and the vegetation. Perhaps he was not conscious of this, but his crude weapons and simple agriculture had no adverse effect on the land or game. The Indian tribes never exterminated any animal or bird. White men have wiped out many, most often through unwise use of agricultural land and wholesale "pest control" projects that backfired.

THE FOX

There are several kinds of "colored" foxes. The breed includes the gray, the black, or silver fox, and the cross fox. The arctic fox and the small kit fox are the pygmies of the family. The swift fox which once roamed the great plains has been exterminated. The gray fox is the only member of the fox clan that can climb a tree without difficulty, and that is an extraordinary canine feat.

The handsome red fox and the color variants that spring from him

Red Fox

is the smallest and most beautiful. The red fox usually has handsome black and white markings such as a white breast, a white tip on his brush, and often, black legs. He uses his brush as a blanket to keep his nose and forepaws warm when lying down. The single yearly litter of a red fox may consist of nine cubs. They are born in a den or burrow, usually during March. One mating may produce normal red foxes and three variants—silver, black, and cross. The red and the gray fox, on the other hand, are distinct species and seldom mate with each other. Both species are widely distributed in North America, but they live apart whenever possible.

The food of all foxes depends on what is available. It includes domestic fowl, rabbits, game birds, songbirds, mice, rats, crayfish, frogs, and beetles. The fox will eat almost anything when hungry, and that includes berries and grapes, some snakes, and vegetables.

Foxes have amazingly keen eyesight, a superb sense of smell, and supersensitive hearing. The distance at which the fox can hear the squeal of a mouse is unbelievable.

It is easy to distinguish the tracks of a fox from those of a dog of similar size. A walking or trotting fox leaves footprints that are almost in line, one behind the other. A dog's tracks are separated left and right and are irregular and staggered.

How Foxes Throw Men and Dogs off the Track

Even after discounting all tall stories about how clever the red fox is,

Red Fox Tracks

it is true that the things he does to avoid pursuit by dogs and men are remarkable. He's an expert at running along the tops of stone walls where dogs often lose his scent. He often crosses and recrosses streams to throw the pack off, and he will even run on a main road where gasoline odors and the smell of rubber deaden the scent he leaves.

Foxes are fond of running along established paths on ridges, cliffs, and the tops of bluffs. The fox has a good lookout from the heights, but he is also taking a chance that an alert rifleman will pick him off as he runs an established route along the skyline or in a place that can be seen from a great distance.

Taking Advantage of Fox Habits

Most of the things that weigh against the wariness and cunning of this bright fellow in red are due to heredity. Foxes follow ancient runways that were used by foxes in the dim past. Though many foxes like to change the site of their dens every year, some foxes persist in using an old den even when many of its inhabitants have been killed while going to or from it. Once a fox has fed well, he seeks out some favorite spot in good cover where he naps and lazes in the sun while he digests his meal. When new snow is on the ground, a hunter may find telltale tracks leading to such a hiding place. The fox is largely a creature of habit and will generally follow the same trail over and over again when foraging. The Indians understood this and often ambushed a wily fox as he followed the well-worn route.

Getting within Range

Very early in the morning or late in the evening, the Indian hunter often took cover downwind from a fox's den to ambush red as he left or returned, and modern hunters sometimes do the same. When a hunter persistently follows the winding trail of a fox in the snow or on damp ground, he may get within range even when using bow and arrow. The fox hears some faint noises made by the cautious hunter, and he cannot go on without doubling back to find out what made the strange sounds. Posting a stander where the pursuit started sometimes works, since the fox often circles back to home ground. Though some of his hunting and marauding is done at night, the fox also hunts and covers a lot of ground during daylight, usually near sunrise and just before dusk.

The presence of a steamy vapor, sometimes frozen into icicles, at the entrance to a fox's den is a sign that at least one fox is within. There is also a musky odor around the entrance of a used den. It is almost impossible to dig a fox out since there is a complex network of passages in a fox's earth when the den has been in use for some time, and there is generally at least one well-concealed bolt hole for emergencies.

Calling

When the fox is sighted coming to the hunter, calling should be continued without a break since the fox is engrossed in his approach and the hunter must keep him curious enough to come right in. Don't stop calling after you bag a fox with a bow since another predator may be approaching the blind from another quarter. After a rifle or shotgun blast, it may be best to move on and take another stand. This is one of the few forms of hunting in which the bowhunter has an advantage.

Fox hunting used to be the exclusive province of those who could hunt with hounds (or with hounds and horses in the European fashion). Now that the art of calling has been rediscovered, fox hunting can be the sport of almost anyone. The caller sits and brings the fox to him with artful sounds as the Indian did. This enables the hunter to hunt many small patches of cover in farm country and on the edges of suburbs.

THE RACCOON

When a white man asked an Algonquin Indian what this animal was called, the Indian said "arakun," and "raccoon" has been his accepted name ever since except when he is called "coon."

It took a while for early settlers to understand the value of the animal, but they learned about it from Indian hunters and trappers. The raccoon is a remarkable animal because he is a predator, a valuable fur-bearer, and an edible animal combined. A big old boar coon is tough and very strong in flavor, but a young one makes a tasty dish, and a prime coonskin is an excellent fur that once brought high prices. Though not expensive now, the quality of the fur has not changed. Among big-game animals, only the young black bear is predator, fur-bearer, and edible. The raccoon resembles the bear in many ways. Both are omnivorous, eating fish, flesh, and vegetable matter.

The raccoon is nocturnal, but sometimes he can be surprised along the banks of streams early in the morning and late at night. A lot of the coon's food (fish and shellfish) comes from the water, and he likes to wash much of his food in fresh water—even if it isn't aquat-

Raccoon

ic fare. A few Indian bowhunters stillhunted coons along streams late in the day and early in the morning, but most of the time the animals were trapped. Sometimes the Indians used their mongrel dogs to tree raccoons at night, but coon hunting with hounds did not become an outdoor art until Europeans arrived with their purebred dogs.

Hunting with Coonhounds

Many specialized strains of "cooners" are known, especially in the South, and a coon hunt with dogs is an exciting experience. Usually the hunters build a fire and sit around it, telling stories of coonhounds past and present mixed with all the racy gossip of the countryside. From time to time, a man steps back from the fire and listens for the

Raccoon Tracks

sound of his own hound or hounds running in the dark woods, and all are conscious of the working pack. Then the hound music rises, indicating a hot chase, and finally the dogs bark "treed."

When all the hunters have gathered, a flashlight is used to locate the coon; someone knocks him out of the tree with a small-bore pistol or rifle, and the fight is on between dogs and the quarry. Sometimes the hunters leash the dogs and take them away, hoping for another chase later on, if no one wants to eat the coon and no one wants the pelt. Hound music on the next hunt is a delightful thing to anticipate. If the dogs are not allowed to kill or maul a coon once in a while, they lose interest in the chase; so most houndmen allow the dogs to chew a little fur occasionally.

A coon is a fairly large animal. An old boar coon may weigh as much as thirty-five pounds, and one lone boar is a good match for a hound or even a pair of them, especially in the water. Coons swim much better than dogs. If a hound follows a coon into deep enough water, the coon usually manages to circle around and holds the dog's head under the water until it drowns. Sometimes the coon mounts the dog's back, the better to use his weight in the fight. Once a dog has been bested by a coon in the water and half-drowned, he often refuses to hunt them again.

Coons are tough, and bowhunters must use broadheaded arrows to kill them. That makes it impossible to release the hounds for their customary fight. A good hound can be injured or killed if he bites down on a broadhead embedded in a coon; so good houndsmen are usually unwilling to work with bowhunters.

Squalling Coons Down from Trees

One peculiarity of coon hunting is squalling. It's difficult to locate the coon in a high tree, when he hides close to the trunk on top of a thick limb. The squaller goes to work either with a manufactured call or his lips and mouth, and makes hideous sounds to make the treed coon believe that there is another on the ground being hurt or killed. If the squaller succeeds, the treed coon may look around to see what is going on, and then someone can get in a shot. Or someone may spot the coon, and see that the animal is treed and has not moved along a limb into another tree. The treed coon may even start down the trunk, apparently to help his nonexistent fellow-coon. Some hunters boast that they can squall a coon down onto the ground if the dogs are held back a little.

Callers working without hounds usually make the high-pitched squawks and excited shrilling of an injured bird early in the morning and late in the afternoon, often near water where they have found coon tracks. Coons rarely respond to the noises that dying rabbits make since the rabbit is seldom hunted by the slow-footed raccoon. If you call, try to sound like a bird common to the area, and you must get the dying sounds into it—a difficult assignment.

THE COYOTE

Despite the inroads of intensive agriculture, coyotes are increasing in numbers and constantly expanding their range. They have invaded southern New England and New York State. Though formerly unknown in Alaska, these animals are now common in some parts of that state. The coyote readily breeds with domestic dogs, the cross being a dangerous game destroyer. Some of these half-breeds are very large, with the natural cunning of the coyote plus the understanding of man that comes from the dog parent. In some states, these coydogs kill many deer, especially fawns and does with young.

The wolflike coyote is a lean, muscular animal about the size of a rather small German shepherd dog. A mature male is about four feet long from nose to tip of tail. His cunning is matched by swiftness of foot. The color of the coyote ranges from gray to nearly black with whitish underparts and a small black tip on the tail. He lives in a

Coyote

burrow similar to that of a wolf, and is far more at home on a grassy plain than in thick brush, though he has adapted to heavy cover in his new territories in the East. His food consists of many things, including rabbits, small rodents, birds, carrion, insects, fruit, and poultry and sheep, when he can get them.

Horseback Hunts

Indian hunters sometimes went after coyotes on horseback for the sake of sport and the animals' coarse, warm fur. A few white men follow the same sport, and the hard riding is sufficient reward. In heavily infested open country, mostly on the prairies and high plains of the West, it is not difficult for a line of riders advancing abreast to put up a coyote or two, especially if there is a fresh fall of snow so that tracks can be seen.

One, two, or even three riders line out after the coyote and push him steadily. This kind of hunting is not as exciting as horseback jackrabbit hunting, but it takes a skilled rider who knows his horse to do it. A coyote in open country usually moves steadily, trying to get away, and does not dodge back among the riders as the big jacks do. When a horse begins to blow and lather or shows other signs of tiring, the rider slows down to a walk, and another follows the track. Sometimes, one rider can run down a coyote by himself, but his horse has to be very good. Finally, the animal is pushed so hard that it must rest, and the nearest rider finishes the hunt with a handgun, or with a club when the hunters want the pelt undamaged. Using a rifle or shotgun as a club is a dangerous practice.

Many coyotes are incidental victims when they fall to a deer or antelope hunter's rifle, and many are shot over the offal of a big-game kill by a hunter who makes it a point to revisit the site a day or two later. Approach quietly downwind and there's a good chance there will be one or more coyotes at the remains.

Vantage Points for Glassing the Country

Stillhunters have little chance to bag a coyote because of the animal's great intelligence and knowledge of home ground, but a few bowhunters have succeeded in this demanding sport. If you can locate a den, you have a better chance. Long-range riflemen often take a stand and glass the country for coyotes before trying a stillhunt, and sometimes they can take the "prairie wolf" from the place

Coyote Tracks

where they sit. Usually a spot where the plain breaks into a river valley, canyon, or wash is best, provided there is some evidence, such as tracks, that the animals are in the area. At these "breaks," the hunter can not only look down into the arroyo or other low ground, but he can also see across the open country near it.

Hunting on Snowshoes and Skis

It is possible to walk down a coyote on snowshoes, though very few men have succeeded in doing so in modern times. When the snow is fluffy and fairly deep, the coyote flounders along but a man on webs can keep up a good pace. If the crust is just right, the coyote may break through it and flounder even more while the hunter's snowshoes spread his weight and permit him to keep going quite fast. Finally, the coyote will stop, and a close-range shot is possible. A few hunters use skis for the sport, and if the snow is right and slopes run in the right direction, the hunter can speedily run the animal down.

THE WOLF

The wolf in North America has a strange history. The Indians occasionally hunted him, and they trapped many of the animals for the sake of pelts, but they never made serious inroads on either the northern timber wolf or the smaller red wolf of the South.

Settler Prejudice

When the white man arrived, the extermination began. European settlers hated the wolf because the animal sometimes destroyed domestic stock, but there was an unrelenting efficiency in the trapping, poisoning, snaring, and wholesale killing of the animal that was almost demonic. One method, used in New England, was to lash three codfish hooks back to back and hang them about six feet off the ground with a chain fastened to a limb. The hooks were baited with meat or offal. The wolf leaped to take the bait and was hooked like a fish and suspended in the air until the trapper came along and killed the animal.

Probably, the settlers reacted to the American wolf violently

Gray Wolf

because of their memories of the European wolf. There is no doubt that in Europe wolves occasionally attacked, killed, and ate people. There is no authentic record of a North American man-eating wolf, and attacks on human beings are so scarce that they can be discounted. That is not to say that rabid wolves have not killed men in this country or that trapped or cornered wolves have not attacked humans, but the North American wolf much prefers to avoid combat with men.

Today, the southern red wolf survives only in eastern Texas, Louisiana, Arkansas, Missouri, and limited areas of Oklahoma. Some members of the species have evidently bred with domestic dogs. The great gray timber wolves of the north are now found chiefly in Canada, though they are present in northern Minnesota in limited numbers. Alaska still has a fairly large wolf population.

Most Effective Hunting Methods

Wolves are occasionally taken by big-game hunters, but few men go after them because they are such difficult animals to hunt. When it is done, it's usually the long-range rifleman who manages to pick one off, often over the remains of a big-game kill. Sometimes, a stillhunter working toward a stander can push a single animal or a small pack out into the open, and then it's usually the stander who gets the shot. Wolves in Alaska and remote areas of Canada are curious and often shadow men just to see what they are doing. Indian hunters were expert at doubling back downwind of their own tracks and getting a shot that way, but it requires skill to do so. It's best to let one or two men go on while another doubles back. Most of the wolves taken today are trapped, poisoned, or shot unsportingly, and sometimes illegally, from aircraft.

In remote areas, the wolf is a valuable predator, and even today, he helps to keep the enormous caribou herds healthy by pulling down and devouring diseased animals. There have been campaigns to give the wolf the status of a game animal with a closed season and a definite limit on the number killed so that the species can be retained, but over most of his remaining range, the wolf is still an outcast to be killed on sight. We may exterminate this American animal by acting

Wolf Print

on the prejudice that was brought to North America from Europe. Our traditional idea of the vicious wolf was wrong. The proof of it is that the primitive Indian did not fear the wolf and neither does the present-day Indian who lives in the wild.

THE WOLVERINE

The Indian attitude toward the wolverine was not one of fear but hatred. Indians called him "The Devil of the Woods," and Eskimos called him "The Evil One." This very large weasel does not attack men unless cornered, though it is very destructive when it feeds along a trap line. The animal follows the line ahead of the trapper and eats every animal caught in the traps or mauls them so badly that the pelts are ruined. Many an Indian trapper still fights wolverines on the trap line, but they are extremely clever and hard to kill and often the trapper is finally forced to pack up and move. Wolverines are also extremely destructive when they break into a food cache or a cabin. Another name for the wolverine is "glutton." Wolverines not only eat all they can but they foul the rest and seem to delight in piercing cans and breaking bottles. One favorite way to eliminate a troublesome member of the wolverine tribe is to put poison in a carcass and leave it out on the trap line, but the wolverine's sense of smell is so keen that it often leaves the poisoned carcass untouched but eats or ruins every other one in the traps.

The wolverine is rarely seen in the United States today, not so much because it was killed off but rather because it is a true wilderness animal which retreats before advancing civilization. A few survive in Washington and along the Rockies down into Colorado and perhaps northern California. The animal's range stretches from the coast of Labrador all the way west to the Pacific in Canada and on into Alaska. It is now mostly an animal of the open Arctic and the belt of "little sticks"—stunted forest along the tree line. A big wolverine may weigh forty pounds, and the color ranges from almost black to a yellowish brown with a pale head.

Its feet are extremely large. The wolverine seems to have the feet and claws of a bear, and the jaws are powerful too. It is said that even a full-grown timber wolf hesitates to tackle the glutton.

The wolverine has poor eyesight, but his excellent hearing and

Wolverine Tracks

keen sense of smell more than make up for it. A wolverine pelt is an unusual and useful trophy for a rifleman; a bowman who manages to bring one down has done something that few Indian hunters managed to accomplish. Wolverine pelts are valued by northern Indians and Eskimos because the fur does not frost, as other pelts do, and it is the favorite fur for lining parka hoods.

THE BOBCAT

The bobcat ranges throughout the United States but few remain in some of the intensively farmed midwestern states. He is a creature of forested lands, broken country, brush, and swamps, though he will live quite close to human beings as many farmers will testify.

The bobcat's fur is usually a bright bay or red-brown color with dark spots and rosettes showing through. The underparts are white. The tail is not bobbed but it is stubby. His ears are tufted, but the tufts are not as large as those of the Canada lynx. His feet are also smaller than the lynx's; so the bobcat cannot navigate on snow as

Bobcat

Bobcat Tracks

well as his northern relative. He is a wiry, muscular animal weighing around thirty pounds, though specimens double that weight have been taken.

The Indians called bobcats, but most of them were taken in traps, because the bobcat's curiosity makes him an easy victim to a clever set.

Hunting with Hounds

Today, the bobcat is hunted with hounds, and in some areas, chiefly in the South, the hunter makes no attempt to kill the animal. If the dogs cannot do it, the cat gets off scot-free. In the North, the hunter usually carries a handgun or a short-barreled rifle or shotgun and tries to get ahead of the hounds. A bobcat runs rather small circles ahead of dogs; so it's often easy for a hunter on foot or on snowshoes or skis to get ahead of the dogs and shoot the cat. If the hunter cannot get ahead of the dogs, the pack will probably tree the cat and hold him until the hunter comes up. Bobcats are largely nocturnal, but dogs sometimes tree one in daylight.

Best Times to Call

The caller has his best chance early in the morning or late in the afternoon, and the agonized squeals of a wounded rabbit or the shrill cries of a bird in trouble work best.

Few hunters go after the Canada lynx because he is scarce in his wilderness range, and most hunters in the far north are after bigger game, but the lynx can be lured by skillful calling.

Many Indian tribes relished the flesh of the cats and ate the bobcat, lynx, and cougar.

THE BIG AMERICAN CATS

The Cougar

The cougar was also called the panther, painter, puma, or catamount, but since his range has been reduced almost entirely to mountain country, the name mountain lion is now most widely used.

The cougar has excellent eyesight, good hearing, and is able to use his nose better than most other cats. In addition to these traits, he is a remarkably silent animal. Some experienced cougar hunters say that they have never heard the animal make a noise except for a little spitting and hissing when angry. The cougar does make a loud noise occasionally but it is a rare occurrence, seemingly triggered by the sex drive. It sounds much like the long drawn out scream of a terrified woman. Because he screams so rarely, the cougar cannot be located by voice, and he is very timid when hunted by men and dogs. The animal will do everything in his power to avoid contact, and his fear of dogs is so great that one small hound can often put him up a tree.

The cougar's chief food is deer. It is said that a mature mountain lion will kill a deer a week. In some areas where conservation practices have brought the deer back in enormous numbers, they do considerable damage to crops and timber and approach the maximum browsing limit beyond which large numbers of them would starve over the winter. One solution would be to reintroduce the cougar, but though that has been proposed from time to time, so far, no eastern conservation department has had the courage to do so.

Many men have lived in western areas for years where there are fairly large numbers of these cats without having seen or heard one. The cougar favors high country and is expert at concealing himself. Where he lives, long stretches of country consist of nothing but bare rock, gravel, and talus. It is almost impossible for a man to follow a cougar's track without a good hound because the tracks are soon lost on a hard stretch. When the animals were more numerous, Indians sometimes managed to call them within bow range by imitating their screaming cries when seeking mates. A fawn's bleat sometimes worked too. Cougars were also killed by ambushing them on their way to and from a known den. Today, however, the cougar has grown so shy and has become so scarce that trying either of these methods is almost hopeless within the United States. A stillhunter who bags a cougar—and it does happen—usually does so by running into one by accident on a deer hunt.

The cougar's weakness ahead of hounds arises from the fact that he has very small lungs. Once the dogs get the cat on the run, the chase may last for only ten or fifteen minutes, and sometimes the cougar trees immediately. The hard work lies in following the cold

Cougar Tracks

trail to the place where the cougar is taking his ease or foraging. Good dogs sometimes work on one cold trail for many hours before they move the cat, and it may take days.

Cougars almost never fight the dogs, but when the animal is shot out of a tree or off a high ledge, the struggles of the wounded cat may maim or kill several valuable hounds.

The Jaguar

The jaguar is a stockier, heavier animal than the cougar and has a much more aggressive nature. There are several authentic records of maneaters among these spotted cats and attacks on hunters are fairly common.

Jaguars are hunted with dogs too, but it is a hazardous business. The jaguar has more staying power, and a considerable number of them refuse to tree. Instead, they turn on the dogs and fight on the ground. The jaguar is capable of killing or crippling all the dogs in even a big pack, one at a time as they overtake him, or several at once as they fall victim to his ferocious fangs and claws. A bayed jaguar often leaves the dogs when the hunter approaches for the kill and attacks the man.

Jaguars can be called. South American Indians can do so with the mouth, sometimes amplified with a horn. A mechanical device is also employed. A big clay pot *(olla)* is used with a strong cord running from side to side through its walls. After rubbing the cord with rosin, the Indian strokes and thrums the cord, and the reverberations in the pot sound like the grunting, coughing sounds that a jaguar makes when foraging at night. Once the jaguar is located through calling, the dogs are put on his track next morning. As with the cougar, it is most difficult for a lone stillhunter to stalk and kill a jaguar.

The jaguar is now almost unknown in the United States, but a few cross the border from Mexico into Arizona—a grim surprise for cougar hounds in the southern part of that state.

9/

Getting Close
To Big Game

WITH ONLY ABOUT 900,000 Indians in what has become the United States and southern Canada, the enormous land area was a tremendous, almost untouched, game preserve into which the European settlers burst. Within this huge wilderness, there were places where even the Indian had not penetrated in any numbers. The Great Plains west of the Mississippi was such an area. This great sea of untouched grassland stretched from the prairie areas of Canada south to Texas and northern Mexico and from the Missouri-Mississippi River system to the foothills of the Rockies. It was full of game, but there was no one to harvest it. Even the Indian tribes seldom ventured out onto the open grassland.

Before the Spanish settlers established themselves along the Gulf Coast and in Mexico and started moving northward in the late 1500s, the western Indians did not have horses. The Indians lived in the foothills of the mountains and along the rivers. They depended mostly on deer and small game for their food. When they moved, their burdens were dragged or carried by their big dogs. The big game of open country, buffalo and antelope, was almost untouched because men needed a swift means of transportation to seek it out and kill it. If the game moved, the Indians could not follow the herd on foot.

By the early 1700s, after the western Indians had acquired horses and had become skilled riders, their way of life changed. During the warm months, they moved out of their sheltered encampments to hunt. In late August and September, the mounted hunters killed buffalo by the thousands and took many antelope to supply winter meat. The flesh was cut into thin strips and dried in the withering heat of the late-summer sun. Together with some deer and elk and perhaps a few mountain sheep and goats killed on high ground in the fall and winter, the buffalo's flesh and the antelope's carried the tribes through to the spring.

Some horses were taken in battle from the Spaniards, others were run off from settlements and ranches, but most of them were strays that wandered northward into the sea of grass. Many northern tribes were unaware of the Spanish to the south. One day, a herd of wild horses appeared on the plains, and a short time later, the Indians were riding them.

Even after obtaining horses, the Indians did not make great inroads on the buffalo. They killed only what they needed for meat and skins with which to make clothing and tepee covers. Armed only with the bow and lance, the Indians harvested less than the natural increase of the herds each season. One single buffalo herd was pretty accurately estimated at 4,000,000 animals by a white frontiersman.

Then the slaughter began. White traders exchanged firearms for hides and furs with the Indians. These weapons, traded from hand to hand, reached into the farthest corners of the plains. With the white man offering guns, powder, lead, tools, trinkets, cloth, and whiskey for buffalo robes and other hides and pelts, many Indians became efficient paid hunters, who were soon joined by professional hunters among the whites who killed even more efficiently. Almost all the buffalo in the United States had been killed by the 1880s, and the antelope neared extinction by the early 1900s.

THE BUFFALO

The American bison is a large, heavy bovine animal with permanent horns and a large shoulder hump. One great bull killed in Kansas is reported to have weighed 3,000 pounds, but 1,900 pounds is about

American Bison

average for a big bull. The wood buffalo, a northern subspecies is even heavier and it is much darker in color. Cow bison are much smaller than bulls.

The great weight of the animal is centered on the front legs and lies mostly in the large hump. The hindquarters, by comparison, are exceptionally small. The shaggy hair and mane on the forequarters and the thick hair of the head provide great warmth. This is why the American bison always faces into a cold wind. Horses, beef cattle, and many others turn their rumps to cold winds. The animal's hide is tough, durable, and makes good leather. Many thousands of hides, tanned in New England, were made into machine belting for the mills of Massachusetts and Connecticut.

How Indians Drove Buffalo on Horseback

The Indians hunted these great animals on horseback. One of their favorite methods was to drive the buffalo over steep cliffs. The mounted men of the tribe searched for a herd of manageable size located near one of these cliffs. Then, shouting, whooping, and riding like demons, the tribesmen charged the lumbering buffalo and tried to stampede them over the precipice. Sometimes it worked, but when the herd stampeded toward the riders and engulfed them, some men and horses were killed. When a herd stampeded toward the hunters, there was only one fleeting chance to escape—race to the side; so, when facing a large, broadfronted herd, the riders' post of honor was always in the center, the point farthest from possible escape to either side. A stampeding herd could swallow up all the mounted men of a tribe.

Once the heavy buffalo began to fall over the cliff, there was no pause until almost all of the animals in a small herd were killed by the fall. Since the animals in the rear could not see the deep drop ahead of them, they pressed forward, driving those in front of them toward the point of no return.

When the last of the herd had been driven over the cliff and a few stragglers that did get through the riders had escaped, hunters and squaws, posted below the cliff, moved in and finished off the crippled animals with killing lances and knives. Then the women began the heavy labor of skinning, butchering, and drying the meat, while the hunters feasted on fresh buffalo tongue, hump, and liver.

When a herd could not be found near a cliff, the Indians were faced with the more dangerous job of milling a herd on the plain. The tribesmen rode fast across the advancing front of the herd, trying to turn the leaders. If it worked, the Indians kept after them until the bison on the outside of the herd were running in a circle, imprisoning those in the center inside a wall of living flesh. Then the killing began.

Riding in a circle on the outside of the milling herd, the horsemen sent arrow after arrow into buffalo after buffalo. Right-handed hunters rode counter-clockwise, shooting to the left. The left-handers rode in the opposite direction, shooting to the right. When the supply of arrows was exhausted, lances came into play. Some tribesmen preferred lances and used them all the time. Though a lance-wielder had to come closer to the dangerous horns and hoofs, it was easier to use a lance on horseback than it was to manage a bow, arrows, and a quiver. The buffalo horses of the hunters were so well trained that they ran in the constantly narrowing circle without guidance from the rider. After the Indians acquired firearms, most of the killing was still done from horseback, but the rider could keep a little farther off and the danger of being trampled was less.

Hunting on Game Preserves

Today, there are probably about 25,000 buffalo in the United States and Canada, many being kept in a semidomesticated state on private ranches and game preserves. The others exist wild on government reserves or in parks, notably Big Delta in Alaska and Wood Buffalo National Park in Canada's Northwest Territories. There is no danger that the buffalo will become extinct, but it is unlikely that its numbers will increase much because of the limited amount of range available for the animal.

From time to time, the herds increase toward the maximum limit under range conditions; then some animals must be shot off. A hunter can still kill a buffalo at Big Delta or Wood Buffalo or on some private preserves if he is willing to pay either the high price charged for the government license or the fees charged by the landowner. Most men who hunt buffalo do so on foot with long-range rifles.

Track of American Bison Walking

THE PRONGHORN ANTELOPE

The pronghorn antelope of the West is a dainty little creature. A good buck antelope weighs about 100 pounds; the does are smaller.

Pronghorn antelope lived among the buffalo herds. Pronghorns often ran among a herd of buffalo to acquire protection from wolves and coyotes that preyed on the young. Though a full-grown, healthy antelope could always outrun a coyote or a wolf, there were times when wolves ran one antelope in relays; then even the bucks needed help. Losing themselves among the bison, the antelope could depend on the predators tangling with the big buffalo bulls or irate cows protecting their own young.

The only other predator the pronghorn contended with before the Indians, then the white men, invaded the prairies was the golden eagle. This large bird often attacked antelope, harrying them to death.

The pronghorn is unique in several ways. He has hollow horns that fit over bony spikes that are integral parts of the skull. This is characteristic of horned animals that keep their horns all their lives. Antlered animals, on the other hand, lose their horns every year, then grow a new set. But the pronghorn has horns, not branched antlers; yet he loses his horns every winter to grow a new set. The horns are also unusual because of the single prong on each that gives the animal its name. Both bucks and does have horns, but the doe's horns are quite small.

The Pronghorn's Signaling System

The pronghorn is tan or light brown in color with a white throat crossed by two dark bars, and white underparts and rump. The pronghorn's hide makes poor rawhide or leather because it is thin, soft, and tears easily. The rump is used as a signalling device. Normally, the brilliant white hairs lie flat, but when the animal is alarmed, the hairs stand up, flaring outward. The antelope usually faces the danger, studying it for a while at a distance in order to determine the nature of the threat and the direction in which it is moving. Then the flaring white rump warns of danger. The signal can be seen for two or three miles across the flat ground. Other antelope face toward the trouble and flare their own rumps. So, the signal radiates outward for miles.

Pronghorn Antelope

The Pronghorn's Senses

The antelope can detect a strange object miles away. Unlike many other wild animals, he seems to be able to spot and classify things that are not moving. Experienced hunters agree that the animal's normal eyesight is equivalent to 8X binoculars.

The antelope has an excellent nose too, and any stalk must be made from downwind or the hunter will never get within range. When alarmed, the pronghorn gives off a musky scent, which also works as an alarm system. The antelope nearest the danger gives off the scent, which the wind carries to others. The antelope usually sees danger before he scents or hears it, but on foggy days or during darkness, this scent-bearing alarm system is very useful.

How Fast Is the Antelope?

Estimates of the animal's speed are usually much exaggerated, but it can sustain a speed of thirty-two miles per hour on level ground for a considerable distance. A blooded racehorse can do thirty-four for some distance; so it is possible for a fine horse to overtake an antelope, though few men have ever been able to ride one down. It has been done, though, by men who owned racehorses for local contests. The hunter jumps out of the saddle at the last moment to make the kill with a handgun or saddle carbine.

Hunting with Gaze Hounds

Very fast greyhounds can catch the antelope too, but it is difficult. Greyhounds and other swift coursing hounds hunt by sight, and are also known as "gaze hounds." The open plains roll just a little, no matter how flat they may look. The antelope is an expert at keeping the slight rises between himself and the hounds and changing direction while out of their sight. If a gaze hound loses sight of the quarry, the dog loses ground and sometimes runs off in the wrong direction. A mounted rider is tall enough to see these switches in direction and urge the hounds on again, but few men were ever fortunate enough to possess both racehorses and very swift gaze hounds.

Pronghorn Antelope Tracks

An Indian Ruse for Taking Antelope

The antelope will run if he sees a man or a predator, and he will do so far out of bow or rifle range. The animal's curiosity, however, sometimes overcomes his skittishness. One method that the Indians used and the white man soon adopted depended on the antelope's inquisitive nature. The Indian hunter lay on his back in a depression, kicking his feet in the air so that the antelope could see them but could not see the Indian's body or head. Overcome by curiosity, a band of antelope would nervously come up to investigate, often retreating, but always returning. Finally, they came so close that there was time for a fast shot with bow and arrow. A tuft of feathers on a thin wand decoyed antelopes too. White men used a white or red rag on a stick.

The antelope has not lost his vein of curiosity, but he has grown cautious. This method seldom works nowadays unless the hunter is in a remote area where the animals have not been hunted much.

The Indian Encirclement Technique

The Indian, in a large band, usually hunted antelope on horseback. A herd was surrounded at long distance with the riders regularly spaced at wide intervals. Then the mounted men rode slowly toward the center. With their enemies coming in from every direction, the antelope became confused, cowered in the center of the circle until it was too late, and could be taken with bows, lances, and even clubs. One traveler who took part in one of these big surrounds just after the Civil War estimated that about 4,000 antelope were killed.

Formerly, white men used the same method, but it is now forbidden by law in almost all the antelope states.

Modern Methods of Standing

Modern hunters often take a stand. The hunter usually lies down on a slight rise so that he is concealed by the high grass and waits until other hunters stir up the animals so that a buck may come close enough for a shot. This type of hunter is usually willing to take any legal male antelope. He has little chance to choose a big buck with trophy-quality horns because chance determines which animals come close to him.

Modern Methods of Stalking

The stalker cruises the plains in a four-wheel-drive vehicle or on horseback until he spots a band. Then he stops to glass them for a good head. If he finds one, he makes his stalk on foot, hands and knees, and belly. Provided the nervous animals stay put long enough (and provided another hunter does not run them off), he may get a shot. Firing at antelope from a moving vehicle or running them down with one so that the hunter can jump out within range and shoot is unsportsmanlike and is usually prohibited by law.

The stalker must leave his vehicle, plan his exact route before starting out, and stay out of sight during the whole approach. With band after band, that may be impossible; so a good antelope hunter does not waste time by trying to make fruitless stalks. He continues to scout until he finds a band where a favorable approach is possible. One hazard of this kind of hunting in areas where the season is open when it is still warm is that the stalker may run into a rattlesnake while crawling on hands or knees or wriggling along on his stomach. In the southern part of the animal's range, cactus is often so troublesome as to make the stalk impossible. The Indian's ability to recognize cactus and other thorned vegetation from a distance is a skill the budding antelope stalker ought to develop.

Even with an accurate, scoped rifle good for 350 or 450 yards, the man who can bring down a *trophy* pronghorn is a skilled hunter.

ELK

The elk or wapiti is an animal of semi-open woodland, though if he's pushed hard by hunters or too much human activity, he retires to thick cover higher in the mountains. The elk once ventured out onto the fringes of completely open grassland, usually along the brushy margins of watercourses. Early western travelers tell us that the elk was so unsuspecting that bands of the animals often approached mounted riders and came right up to wagons.

The Indians hunted them, sometimes with dogs, but most often by stillhunting. Indians killed few elk. Wolves and coyotes pulled down the young and the sick, but a bull or cow elk is so large and powerful that it usually took several predators working together to do the job. The bull stands five feet high at the shoulders. He may weigh as much as 1,000 pounds. To men who hunt the whitetail deer, those are impressive figures. At most, a good whitetail buck stands 3 feet 10 inches tall and weighs about 300 pounds. This differential makes it difficult for eastern hunters to estimate range. The elk is so much larger than the whitetail that the hunter often underestimates the range and shoots low.

Finding the Herd

The Indian elk hunter relied on his horse to find the animals, as some modern hunters do. Though elk have taken to higher ground and denser cover, they have not given up their wandering habit. A band of elk hidden in some brushy draw may be ten or twelve miles away the following morning. As a result, packhorses and saddlehorses must be used to find them unless the hunter is a local man who knows the habits of the elk well. The usual practice is to ride ridges and other high ground, pausing now and then to glass the country. When a band of elk is sighted, the hunter rides as close as he can, then dismounts and stalks the herd bull. Sometimes a system of standers and drivers can be used. The standers are posted on one side of a patch of cover, downwind from it, while mounted men circle round and push the animals to them.

Elk Whistles

Lone hunters often rely on calling. Either a homemade or a manufactured elk whistle is used to imitate the burbling, whistling call of a bull elk trying to attract cows and warn off rivals. When the caller gets an answer, he may be able to repeat the calls and bring the bull right up to his stand, but quite often the animal detects some imperfection in the call and runs. Then the hunter knows that there is a bull elk in the area which he may be able to stalk later on. In some states, the season is not yet open when the rut is already in progress. A number of hunters bring their elk whistles along on early small-game

Bull Elk

hunts and call from time to time. They get answers and so learn the general area where the elk are located. When the season opens, it's possible to guess with fair accuracy where elk are. Very large, old bulls with trophy racks seem to lose some of the elk's wandering ways. At any rate, they usually stick pretty close to heavy cover.

Typical Elk Terrain

Elk are browsers and grazers. They like twigs and leaves from low bushes and trees, but they also like to graze on fresh green grass. To do so, they must come out into the open "parks" in the foothills of

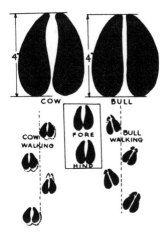

Elk Tracks

the mountains. Wise elk are shy of doing that after the hunting season starts; so they are likely to be found on open patches of grass only early in the morning and toward evening. The larger animals do not stray very far out into the open.

If you see cows and calves in the open, sit down and study the tree fringe near them foot by foot, slowly. The herd bull may be hidden just a little inside the edge.

In the middle of the day, the stillhunter has to penetrate heavy cover for elk. That's the time when a system of standers and drivers works best.

Range

At one time, the elk's range included almost every state in what has become the Union. Many were killed in Pennsylvania during Colonial times. They ranged from high country down almost to sea level. Today, only a few western states have open seasons. The elk has been reintroduced into a few eastern states, and Pennsylvania and Virginia have had fairly substantial herds for many years. Virginia has even had a few open seasons.

The problem with the elk is that they are insatiable feeders. They strip fruit trees and valuable berry bushes when wild feed runs out or is snowed over or frozen. A band of elk can also destroy wheat, rye, and oats at an astonishing rate, not only by eating it but also by trampling it. Most farmers protest the reintroduction of large numbers of elk.

MOOSE

The moose is a tremendous creature. When a man sees a full-grown bull for the first time, a common feeling is that the animal is a survival from prehistory and "impossible." An Alaskan bull moose may weigh as much as 1,800 pounds and stand as tall as 7½ feet at the shoulders. The astonishing thing about the animal is the great height from ground to tips of the great palmated antlers—8 to 10 feet. This huge animal is "the great deer," and many Indian names for him incorporate that idea. The moose's snout, which overhangs the front of his mouth, is almost prehensile. He uses the soft pad of tissue to sweep twigs into his mouth. Then he holds them against his teeth, and pulls his head away, stripping them of bark and leaves, but the bark is stripped away only on one side of the twig or branch. If you find freshly stripped twigs, bare only on one side, a moose is nearby. In addition to bark and twigs, this great animal loves succulent water vegetation, often submerging in the water to get at it. In summer, ticks, flies, and mosquitoes attack moose furiously; so the animal often submerges to escape them, only his head held above water for air, and he plunges that below the surface frequently, to defeat the tormenting insects.

A fisherman who travels wilderness lakes and streams in Canada may see many moose as he moves along silently in his canoe, but when the fall cold sets in, killing the insect pests off, the animal moves back into drier country away from the lakes and streams. The Indian was not restrained by closed seasons; so he often killed the big animals while they were almost completely submerged in the water, sometimes with bow and arrow, often with a lance wielded from a canoe. The moose is easy to kill when in water.

In low-lying country, shoreline vegetation is often so heavy that a hunter moving in the thick cover would make so much noise that it would be impossible to stalk the animal. The moose has excellent hearing, a good sense of smell, but poor eyesight. Yet, moose do not

Moose

seem to realize that traveling with the wind can be dangerous. Moose often move along with the wind blowing on their rumps, browsing as they go; so Indian moose hunters often took advantage of this by circling around and waiting until the moose came close enough for a shot with bow and arrow. Modern hunters can sometimes do the same.

Calling with a Birchbark Horn

Another Indian method of moose hunting still works well. In calling, the hunter uses a large roll of birchbark in the form of a megaphone to focus and magnify the calls he makes with mouth and throat. The caller imitates the sound made by a cow, which somewhat resembles the frantic lowing of a domestic cow.

Calling is often done from a canoe in areas where the moose do not retreat from the water during the cool season. When the bull answers and begins to move forward, the canoe is silently paddled along the shore until the hunter in the bow can get a shot. If a bull is shy and hesitates to come in, the caller may imitate the harsher, more guttural sounds of another bull to give the quarry the impression that he has a rival in the area. Sometimes it works, and the angry bull throws caution to the wind and charges close to the hunters. Some callers also use a sponge or ball of dry moss to drip water suddenly over the side of the canoe. When the rut is on, moose seem to urinate a great deal, and copiously. The sound attracts them. Canoe hunting is practiced mostly in eastern Canada, where moose inhabit swampy, stream-crossed areas.

Using Binoculars

In the West and in much of Alaska, moose hunters usually glass the great animals from a rise of ground or a tree. When a hunter spots a trophy bull, he plans his stalk carefully, comes down, and makes his try. Of course, the animal is out of sight as soon as the hunter is on level ground again; so he may make many stalks before a bull stays put long enough for him to close in and take the shot or photograph.

Moose live in thick cover, are rather scarce over much of their range, and are remarkably adept at concealing themselves and ghosting away from hunters. Therefore, driving moose between standers and drivers rarely works and is seldom tried.

It is amazing that such an enormous creature can fade away so silently in the woods. One expects that this great, seemingly awkward animal would make much noise, but he can pick his way silently and quickly. The dark, brownish black hide blends deceptively with dark tree trunks, and the legs themselves look very much like the lower portions of saplings. When there is snow on the ground, however, the dark animal stands out more clearly.

Why the Moose Is Dangerous

Some hunters say that there are two dangerous kinds of game in North America—the big western bears and the moose. Many hunters and other outdoorsmen have been killed by moose; sometimes the bull is so driven by the frenzy of the rut that he will charge anything that annoys him. When moose first see a human being, they often stand and stare at the man for a while before running off. Some observers say that this is due to a low-level nervous system that reacts slowly. Others believe that the bull is contemplating an attack. Most of the time, the moose tries to fade away, but sometimes, especially during the rut, the animal will make an all-out charge. Cows are less belligerent, but if a cow has young nearby, she can be nearly as dangerous as the bull.

Like all other North American deer, the moose uses his antlers in fights with rival males. Since his long legs give him a long reach, when fighting wolves, man, and other predators, the moose uses his sharp-pointed front hoofs, which can disembowel a man in one stroke.

A wounded moose can be very dangerous. It takes a well-placed bullet to drop a moose in his tracks. Some hunters try to break the neck or the shoulders much as in bear hunting on the theory that it's best to put potentially dangerous game down first, then kill with a second shot. Others try for the heart-lung area. If a wounded moose runs off, the hunter should be most cautious when following it.

Once the moose ranged down into the United States in New England, New York, and in the lake states. The moose population along the backbone of the Rockies was also once quite large. Today, moose have been exterminated throughout New England except in

Walking *(left)* and Running *(right)* Moose Tracks

Maine, and some survive in the northern Rockies. Only a few western states have open seasons. The largest moose are found in Alaska and Yukon Territory. This far-northern form of the animal has been recognized as a separate subspecies along with the Canadian moose (southern and eastern Canada) and the Shiras or Wyoming moose, a smaller race inhabiting the Rocky Mountains in Idaho, Montana, and Wyoming.

Hunting the moose is a rare privilege for the few who can afford guides and packtrain hunting, and can spare the time usually required to travel to and from a remote area and find a good trophy. After bagging a bull moose with a high-power rifle, imagine doing it with a crudely made bow and arrow such as the Indians used. Almost always, a single arrow failed to kill; so the Indian hunter had to follow along in thick cover so that he could shoot arrow after arrow into the great beast. If you bowhunt for moose, your guide will almost always remain close by with a rifle or wisely insist that another hunter do so.

CARIBOU

In the far northern herds of caribou, one can see what the great herds of plains game must have been like before the coming of the white man. Thousands of the animals roam the open Arctic country in huge herds, moving southward as snows begin to pile up deeply, covering the stunted vegetation and moss on which they feed. Caribou inhabit the Canadian and Alaskan Arctic and sub-Arctic from Newfoundland all the way to the Alaska peninsula. At one time, the range extended into southern New England and New York. The animals were recently reintroduced in Maine, but the herd is not prospering.

Three races of caribou are recognized: woodland, mountain, and the barren-ground. The woodland and mountain caribou are more like deer and moose in their habits. They have largely abandoned open country, and having better browse available, they do not migrate over the great distances that the barren-ground caribou covers. The man who can hunt deer successfully will have little difficulty when hunting any form of caribou, and much the same methods are used with the woodland and mountain subspecies.

Indian and Eskimo Drives

When hunting the barren-ground caribou, the problem is to be in the right place at the right time to pick out a suitable trophy. The animals move southward in September and October. That's when the Indians and Eskimos killed them in large numbers for winter meat. Often big drives were organized either on foot or using dogs and sleds. The big surrounds often gave the Indians the opportunity to kill hundreds of caribou in a short time, much as antelope were killed farther south by the Plains Indians.

Caribou

The open wastes of the barren ground do not differ much from plains country to the south as far as hunting is concerned. Some of the barren ground, however, is muskeg; if the weather is still warm during the season, the hunter must be prepared to wade marshy ground. Usually, tufts of thick grass provide fairly solid footing, as the hunter

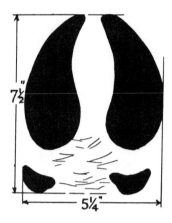

Caribou Print

leaps from one tuft to another. If you miss your step and go into soft muskeg, you'll probably sink up to the waist and stick there for a while. Many a stalk has been ruined because the hunter took one misstep and could not get out of the mire quickly enough to shoot the bull of his choice. Keep your rifle high if you go in. Getting the muck off the action of a gun and out of the barrel so that it will function and not blow up wastes much time.

As the native hunters knew, even a big lake or a wide river is not a barrier to caribou; so it's impossible to use one as a backstop when stalking. When driven by one or more hunters, the animals enter the water and swim off, no matter how cold or wide the water is. Caribou are very buoyant, because each hair is hollow; the animals float high in the water, and swim strongly. On the big Eskimo and Indian drives, entire herds were sometimes forced into the water and killed there with lances wielded from canoes and kayaks. The wind usually pushed the buoyant carcasses quickly to shore. Today, killing caribou in the water is prohibited except by native hunters in certain remote districts.

When barren-ground caribou are moving along in search of food and shelter, the herd moves rapidly until it finds them. When the sparse vegetation is exhausted, sometimes after only a short stay, the animals move again. Because of this, the hunter may not see a single animal one day and be in the midst of thousands the next. Studying stripped and damaged vegetation, particularly the purplish caribou moss, will tell you if a herd has moved through recently.

Locating and Stalking a Trophy Animal

The caribou hunter usually glasses from a height (if one can be found) until he locates a trophy animal. Then he makes his stalk. Caribou are remarkably trusting animals. They behave much as plains game must have before they were heavily hunted. Often, the hunter can move alongside a herd without spooking the animals, provided the man stays downwind from them. The sight of a hunter does not alarm the animals much, and the caribou's eyesight is poor. Scent is much more likely to send them off. There's little chance to spook caribou by noise on the open, treeless barren ground.

The problem is to shoot the trophy bull without putting a bullet into a cow or a yearling. There always seems to be one or more other animals between the hunter and the chosen target. Yet, if the hunter gets too close, they will spook; the bull also. Sometimes it pays to sit down and wait where there is a little cover, perhaps behind a low rise. In their aimless wandering as they feed, the animals cover a lot of ground; so a clear shot at the trophy animal may open up suddenly. Since both cows and bulls have antlers, a hunter should take a moment to check before firing to be sure that his sights are really on the big, trophy bull—not on a big cow. The Indians did not have this problem since they hunted for meat and hides, not a trophy rack. They preferred to take cows and young animals because their meat was more tender.

Indian Trick for Getting within Range

If the caribou are jittery, it may be difficult even to get within rifle range of the herd. To get within bow range, primitive Indians and Eskimos sometimes used a very simple trick, taking advantage of the caribou's poor vision and its inability to count. Two hunters stood close together and walked toward the herd. Their legs moved in unison, one behind the other; so to the feeding animals, they looked much like a lone man. As long as the hunters were at some distance, the animals did not run. The two hunters moved forward until they reached a low rise or some other cover chosen in advance. There the man with the bow took cover and readied his tackle while the other hunter moved off in plain view of the caribou. To the animals, all danger seemed past. They continued to move forward toward the concealed hunter, who got an easy shot at close range. This method can still be used to take a trophy animal.

The caribou is not a large animal. At most, a big barren-ground bull stands 3½ feet high at the shoulder and weighs about 375 pounds. The mountain and woodland races are often larger, though they too may be small if they live in a region where browse is scarce.

MULE AND COLUMBIA BLACKTAIL DEER

In addition to the whitetail deer, previously discussed, there are two other species of deer in the United States—the mule deer of the West and the Columbia blacktail deer of the Pacific slope—both hunted by the Indians.

Distinguishing the Mule Deer from the Whitetail

The mule deer, usually larger than the whitetail, has branched antlers. Since the main beam of an antler forks equally, and the two forks branch again, the normal number of points on a mature mule deer's rack is generally four on each side. When there are additional points, they usually branch off this main structure. The whitetail's main beam sweeps outward, then curves forward, and all the points branch off the main beam. The mule deer got his name because of his enormous ears, much larger than a whitetail's, but there are other differences that can be used as field marks. This is sometimes very important, because the range of the whitetail and the mule deer overlap in a wide area and in some places the season on one animal may be closed while the other may be legal game.

The whitetail's large white flag is characteristic. The mule deer has a long, ropelike tail with a black tip. When the mule deer is going away, his tail is carried low, pressed against his rear. The whitetail's flag is carried high when the deer is running, with the white underside plainly visible.

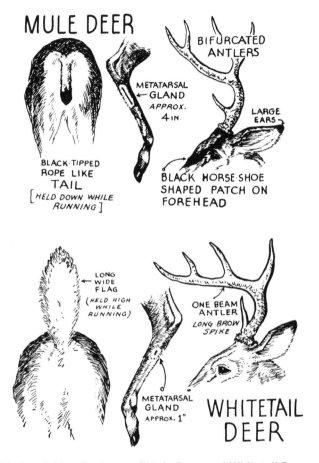

MULE DEER

BIFURCATED ANTLERS

METATARSAL GLAND APPROX. 4 IN.

LARGE EARS

BLACK-TIPPED ROPE LIKE TAIL [HELD DOWN WHILE RUNNING]

BLACK HORSE-SHOE SHAPED PATCH ON FOREHEAD

LONG WIDE FLAG (HELD HIGH WHILE RUNNING)

ONE BEAM ANTLER LONG BROW SPIKE

METATARSAL GLAND APPROX. 1"

WHITETAIL DEER

Distinguishing Features of Mule Deer and Whitetail Deer

Capitalizing on the Mule Deer's Curiosity

Hunting methods for mule deer resemble those used for elk. In open country, the mule deer is often spotted from high ridges, and hunters move along on horseback while scouting. Mule deer are generally said to be less adept at avoiding hunters than the whitetails. Hunters often say that the mule deer surrenders to curiosity while the whitetail never does. In remote areas, the mule deer will often run off some distance, then pause for one final look at the hunter. That's when it's important to have the rifle ready. Some hunters count on this habit. They will not shoot when the mule-deer buck is running away. Instead, they sit down or lie prone, take a good rifle rest, and wait until the animal pauses to look back.

Mule deer, once animals of the low foothills, often ventured out onto the open plains. Before the coming of the white men, they were trusting creatures, easily killed at short range in open country with the Indian's crude archery tackle. Even today, the mule deer is much more apt to feed out in the open grassy parks and cross open ground than the whitetail deer or the Columbia blacktail, but the same thing that happened to much other North American game is happening to the mule deer. They are growing more wary as population and hunting pressure increases. Sitting near the heads of open canyons, or waiting for mule deer to come out of cover, has grown less profitable. Since mule deer have become familiar with men and rifles, they no longer pause so often to look back at a man.

As a result, mule-deer hunting is changing; many mule-deer hunters are learning to imitate the whitetail hunter of the East. They find that it is now necessary to go into thick cover on foot after the mule deer, particularly if the target is a big buck. During the hunting season, a big old buck may lie up in thick cover near water and stay there the entire time. When possible, the animal selects a hide on a height where he can look over a wide stretch of country and spot approaching hunters at a distance. If he does spot a hunter, he'll sneak out by the back door before the hunter is within range. In some areas, hunters work in pairs, one man circling around behind a likely patch of cover while another approaches in plain view. What is more, some hunters are now driving mule deer.

If you want to hunt mule deer in the traditional way, you have to make a long packtrain trip to a remote area, probably up near the timber line. A few states have special early seasons so that hunters can get at these big mule-deer bucks before snow closes the high country to travel. Since even in the high country, the pressure on the mule deer is increasing, it may not be many years before mule-deer hunters will be studying the methods developed by the Woodland Indian of the East to hunt the whitetail, described in Chapter 4.

Identifying the Columbia Blacktail

The Columbia blacktail deer is smaller than a mule deer. It resembles the whitetail in both habits and appearance. Again, the tail is a field mark for the hunter. The tail is not as large as a whitetail deer's, though the shape is similar. When the blacktail is not alarmed, the tail is down; so its rear surface is almost entirely black. There is only a thin white margin around the edges.

Range of the Columbia Blacktail

The Columbia blacktail is confined to the western slope near the Pacific from Sitka, Alaska to Southern California; therefore the blacktail's range barely overlaps that of the whitetail in very few places.

The blacktail deer is an animal of forest margins, low scrub, swamps, and thickets. Because he inhabits much the same kind of country, hunting methods for the blacktail closely resemble those used when hunting whitetail deer.

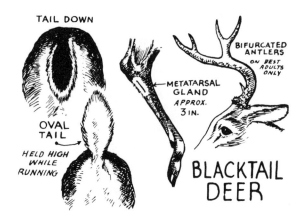

Distinguishing Features of Columbia Blacktail Deer

THE BLACK BEAR

Range

The first bear sighted is usually a black bear, often considered an eastern animal. Though this animal is a creature of the woods, his range is not restricted to the East. It extends from coast to coast in Canada, down the coast ranges, the Rockies, and along the Appalachians, south to Florida. Originally, only the plains states and those with large arid areas lacked the animal, but it has been killed off in a few states where it once was common. Still, almost any hunter in the United States can hunt black bear with good hope of success if he is willing to travel only a short distance.

Weight

The black bear is usually harmless, though he is equipped with powerful claws and teeth and sometimes grows to enormous size. There

Black Bear

are legends of 1,000-pound black bears. The great Canadian-American naturalist Ernest Thompson Seton related that he had heard of a black bear weighing over 900 pounds that was killed in Arizona in 1921. Average weight for a mature animal is about 300 pounds.

Color Variations

The black bear is not always black. It may be reddish, bluish, brown, yellow, and white in the rare subspecies known as Kermode's bear found in British Columbia. The difference between the black bear and the grizzly lies not so much in color and build as in temperament. If in doubt about a certain bear, two physical characteristics tell the story: the grizzly has a large hump over his forequarters, but the black bear has none; the grizzly has a pug-nose snout between nostrils and eyes but the black bear has an arched, rather prominent snout.

Hunting Methods of the Woodland Indians

The temperamental difference between the black bear on the one hand and the grizzly, Alaska brown bear, and the polar bear on the other is vast. Though the black bear is a powerful, well-armed animal, he is normally very shy and fears man and dogs. The other bears are much more aggressive.

The difference is demonstrated by the hunting methods of the primitive Indians and Eskimos. The Woodland Indians of the East and many western tribes did not fear the black bear and stillhunted him much like deer. The Indian was not afraid to crawl into a black bear's den and dispatch him there with nothing more than a spear or even a hand ax. The grizzly was feared by the Indians and, as a rule, wasn't hunted. On the rare occasions when the Indian did hunt the grizzly, a large party went after the animal, and horses were often used so that the hunters could keep clear of the bear.

Many western tribes had a superstitious fear of the great grizzly bear. This fact was brought out when the U.S. Forest Service began putting up "Smokey the Bear" signs in Indian areas visited regularly by tourists. The Indians respected the Forest Service's desire to prevent fires, but their ancient superstitions warned them it is bad luck to look upon a grizzly bear, and Smokey looks more like a grizzly than a black bear. Therefore, the Indians cut the picture of the bear out of the posters but left them in place. The message was good, but the Indians saw no need to spoil their luck by looking at Smokey.

The first reaction of a black bear to the sound of a shot is to run away. The grizzly may run too, but he sometimes turns toward the sound of the shot, runs right over the hunter, and may tear and maul him.

Dangers to Man

The big black is also not an animal to trifle with. There are many reliably reported cases in which the black bear has pulled down and killed a man. Such things usually happen when the animal is cornered or is wounded so that flight is impossible, but there have been occasions when black bears have attacked people without provocation and killed them, and there are a few instances in which the black bear ate the victim. The grizzly attacks much more often than the black bear, but cases in which the grizzly devoured the victim are rare.

Any sow bear with cubs is dangerous, even a black. Anyone who places himself between any bear cub and the sow is risking his life, and to pick up a bear cub and handle it in the woods is extremely dangerous.

The black bear will eat anything from ant grubs to moose and deer, provided he can locate a young or sick animal. The black bear, like most other bears, cannot catch fast-moving animals.

Tree-climbing Ability

The black bear can climb, but large blacks seem to avoid climbing trees even when pursued by dogs. That may be because they prefer to fight dogs on the ground rather than climb. The bear seems to have learned that once he is treed by the dogs, a hunter may soon be along with a rifle. The grizzly and the Alaska brown do not climb trees even when they are young, and there are no trees for the polar bear to climb.

How Males Stake Out Their Territory

Most black bears taken in the eastern states are shot by accident. A deer hunter happens to come across old blackie by surprise and shoots. The black bear is such a stealthy creature and so adept at avoiding man that it is almost hopeless for the lone stillhunter to go after him unless he feels certain, from tracks or other sign, that there is one in the area. The black bear, together with the grizzly, leaves sign for other bears by clawing a tree as high up as he can reach when standing on his hind legs. The theory is that the bear shows his height by scratching as high as possible. If another bear cannot reach higher, he is outmatched and will not try to settle in that particular patch of cover. To advertise the "bear tree," the bear urinates profusely nearby, and the smell attracts other bears for a look-see at who else is present in the area. The sign and the smell may also attract a mate. If you find such a bear tree and see tracks nearby, the chances are good for a shot or a photograph.

Black Bear Tracks

Indian Method of Baiting

The Indians sometimes baited black bears with the entrails of deer or some other ripe meal. It was staked out in an open area which bears were using, and the Indian hunter took his stand in heavy cover or a blind downwind from the bait. When the bear appeared, the Indian attacked with bow and arrow and perhaps followed up with a lance. Today, riflemen use the same system for black bears, particularly in the thick evergreen cover of southern Quebec and Maine. Grizzlies are sometimes baited too.

Hunting with Hounds

Black bears are also hunted with hounds. The chase can be long and even dangerous. Young bears will almost always tree, and the hunter takes the shot almost straight up. A big, wise old black bear doesn't climb. If the bear has been run before, he knows that he must fight the dogs on the ground to escape. Bruin hopes to put the pack out of action so that the kill can never be made. Dogs cannot kill bears on their own. If you ever face this situation, get there fast or the bear will almost certainly kill many valuable hounds. A bear-hound fight is no place for an archer. An instantaneous kill is needed; so a heavy rifle must be used. Even then, dogs are sometimes terribly mauled or killed because the hunter cannot get a clear shot that would not injure a dog. Guides who hunt bear with good dog packs have little respect for a bear hunter who cannot get there fast with a gun.

THE GRIZZLY BEAR

Dogs are not used to hunt the fierce grizzly bear because the animal would turn on the pack and kill them all or run them out of the country, though a few early hunters did hunt grizzlies with packs when dogs were not as valuable as they are today. Some hunters used one good strike dog on leash to locate the bear and bring the man close to the quarry. Then the dog was tied, and the hunter went in with his rifle. Grizzlies are usually baited or stillhunted nowadays.

Grizzly Bear Prints *(left:* **hind foot,** *right:* **front foot)**

Hunting Vaquero-Style with Lariats and Lances

In early times, grizzlies were so common in the West that they invaded the plains, especially in the southwestern states. The Indians left them alone, but the Spanish-American vaqueros of California and Mexico, many of whom had Indian blood, took pride in their method of handling the grizzly. They used lariats and stretched the bear out between them, dallying the ropes to their saddle horns and using the weight and strength of their horses. The bear was then killed with a cattle lance or taken to a town for a favorite Spanish-American amusement—a contest in an arena between the bear and a big longhorn bull. The bear usually killed the bull outright with one blow of a paw at the head or neck that snapped the spine.

Hunting with Bow and Arrow

Grizzlies have been killed by archers using modern hunting bows and broadheaded arrows. Sometimes only one arrow was needed. In this, the modern bowhunter somewhat excels in prowess his Indian predecessor, who rarely attempted to kill a grizzly with a bow and arrow. The modern archer usually plays safe and goes after the big bears accompanied by a guide or another hunter armed with a big-bore rifle as backup gun.

SPOTTING AND STALKING
THE ALASKA BROWN BEAR

The Alaska brown bear has also been taken by archers. This bear lives mostly on the coast of Alaska and British Columbia or on the offshore islands. These bears were not discovered by science until 1896, when they were first described and classified. The big brown bear is essentially a grizzly adapted for life on the coast, where the principal food is fish. The great bear fattens up on salmon before hibernating in the fall, and the spring finds him just existing on a restricted diet of berries, marmots, and other small mammals. He may also kill and eat young deer and cripples, and he will eagerly devour any animal that cannot escape him.

Alaska browns live in treeless country where the vegetation consists of tall grass, low scrub such as alders, and dwarf willows. Over the centuries, the bears have worn deep trails, which often resemble tunnels. They pass through the thick, low scrub and are worn so deep that the branches form a roof over them. Indian-style stalking by

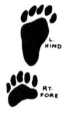

Alaska Brown Bear Tracks

walking or crawling along these trails often brings a hunter within reach of a bear, but sometimes the bear comes upon the hunter unexpectedly, occasionally from the rear, when the hunter may be in an awkward position where he cannot use his rifle for a quick shot. Such things have happened, and the encounter is often fatal to the man.

Often, the hunter sits downwind of the trail at a point where the scrubby cover is sparse or absent and hopes to take his bear as bruin moves along the trail. Hunters sometimes find it profitable to follow salmon streams inland by wading because the surrounding cover is so thick that movement in it could betray the hunter far in advance of his approach.

Sometimes it is possible for the hunter to cruise the beaches of saltwater inlets in a boat and spot the Alaska brown before going ashore to hunt him. This method is less successful now since the bears are growing shy of showing themselves near salt water.

Bears are often hunted in the spring just as they emerge from their dens after hibernation. At that time, as the Indians well knew, their pelts are in prime condition. In the fall, the bear often rubs his hide against trees and rough boulders to shed hair; so large "rubs" (bare patches) appear in the pelt that ruin it as a trophy.

THE POLAR BEAR

Polar bears are very large animals four feet high at the shoulder, and males have been recorded at 800 pounds. The polar bear has not grown used to man. Instead of displaying the trusting attitude of the caribou, though, this bear is often aggressive and seems to regard a human being as nothing else than some kind of odd seal—easy game to catch and eat. The Alaska brown and the grizzly will attack if pushed too hard, but they seldom deliberately stalk a man to kill him. The polar bear is different. It often stalks man, and Eskimos have many superstitious beliefs about the supernatural viciousness of the animal. When Eskimos do hunt polar bears, they shoot them when they are swimming—an unsporting kill—or release sled dogs to harry and circle the bears until the hunters can get in a shot. Eskimos do not hunt polar bears regularly, but polar bears are shot when accidentally found during seal and walrus hunts.

Polar Bear   **Polar Bear Tracks**

The polar bear population of the American and Canadian Arctic has been greatly reduced by hunters who use airplanes to locate the animals. Once a trophy bear is spotted from the air, the plane lands on skis, and the hunter takes his bear by stalking or sitting for him along his line of advance. Care has to be taken not to become the hunted. The bear has good eyesight, hearing, and nose. He sometimes spots the hunter first, circles around, and takes the man from the rear. A good guide always keeps a close watch to the hunter's rear to make sure that this does not happen.

The Boone and Crockett Club is no longer awarding record status and listing in their "Records of North American Big Game," for trophy polar bears. There has been so much abuse in hunting this bear by airplane that the club is awaiting strongly enforced legislation and more sportsmanlike practices. It has been reliably reported that the airplane is often used to haze the bear to the waiting hunter. Present regulations forbid this unsportsmanlike method of hunting.

MOUNTAIN SHEEP AND MOUNTAIN GOATS

The mountain sheep and the mountain goat are two of the most difficult animals to hunt in North America, and the hunting can be dangerous. It is not that the animals attack the hunter; rather, the high country fights for them. Many hunters have been severely injured or killed on mountain hunts for these animals when attempting climbs that were too strenuous.

The mountain goat has black, slightly curved, spikelike horns. The sheep has curled horns that resemble those of the domestic ram. The goat is actually not a true goat, but a kind of specially adapted antelope; so he does not resemble the domestic goat in body outlines.

Bighorn Sheep

Mountain Goat

The heavy, spiralling horns of the mountain sheep make a much more impressive trophy than the horns of the goat; so they are prized more by hunters. The meat of the mountain sheep is considered by many hunters to be the world's best wild meat. The meat of the wild goat is stringy and tough, and is not usually eaten.

Even though a guide may help the sheep hunter, the sportsman himself must also be very skilled. It is he who makes the final stalk, and does the shooting. He must also be tough enough to travel long distances and climb in the thin air of the high country.

Both males and females among the wild sheep and goats have horns, but the horns of the female mountain sheep are small and

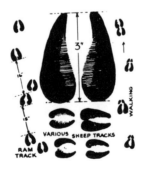

Mountain Sheep Tracks

spiky, in no way comparable to those of the magnificent ram. The female mountain goat's horns may be just as long as a billy's, but they are usually much thinner. It is sometimes difficult to tell the female goat from the ram at a distance, but there is seldom any doubt regarding sheep.

Rocky Mountain Bighorn Sheep

Though there are many strains of mountain sheep, hunters lump them all together under four main classifications.

The wild sheep with the widest geographical range is the Rocky Mountain bighorn. The range extends from southern Canada along the Rocky Mountains, far south almost into Mexico. This sheep and the more southerly desert bighorn were once found on isolated patches of high ground, mesas, and buttes out on the open plains and in the low foothills of the high mountains. As hunting pressures and competition for food by domestic sheep increased, these isolated pockets of wild sheep were eliminated, and the animal retreated to the high mountains. This condition has affected northern sheep too, but to a lesser degree.

The Rocky Mountain bighorn is a brown sheep. Big rams are as long as six feet, with a heavy, well-fleshed body. Weight runs up to 300 pounds, and the horns are the largest in bulk of all the American sheep.

Desert Bighorn Sheep

The desert bighorn is essentially a Rocky Mountain bighorn reduced in size because of the arid country in which he lives. Color and conformation are much the same, but total bulk of the animal and the horns is less. The desert sheep inhabits high country in northern Mexico and the more arid, mountainous parts of the Rockies in the Southwest.

Stone Sheep

The Stone sheep is often called the black sheep because its pelage is so dark. Though some forms shade off into creamy color, that color phase is caused by a mixture of black and white hairs, not by individual buff-colored hairs. These sheep are confined to the area at the headwaters of the Stikine River, British Columbia, and the region north and east of there.

Dall Sheep

The Dall is an Alaskan. He is also called the white sheep. In the northern part of the state, Dalls inhabit the Brooks Range. These animals are rather small. In south-central Alaska, another and larger race of Dalls inhabits high ground. The Dall is unique among the wild sheep because his coat is a pure, glistening white, contrasted sharply with the glossy black of the hoofs. The Dall has thinner horns than our other wild sheep, and the sharp, finely molded horns make a magnificent, graceful trophy.

Taking a good specimen of all four North American sheep is called a Grand Slam among hunters, and the man who has achieved it has a right to be proud of his hunting prowess. The desert ram is scarce and also the hardest to take because of the high, arid country in which he lives.

Indians hunted sheep too, but their kills must have been few. Without binoculars and long-range rifles, hunting mountain game proved to be very difficult. A point in the Indian hunter's favor is the fact that the wild sheep frequented lower country more often before the coming of the white man. The most common Indian method was to surround an isolated butte or mesa out on the plains where sheep were known to be. The sheep were driven to the peak of the rise. (This could also be done on rather low foothills of the high mountains, provided there was no saddle connecting the height with another hill or if the saddle was well covered with a line of hunters.) The Indians were hunting for meat, not trophy horns; so they were much more likely to shoot lambs, ewes, and young rams than old trophy animals.

Stalking Mountain Sheep

The sheep hunter commonly depends on a native guide and a pack-train to get him into sheep country and place him where it may be possible to take a trophy ram. Then binoculars and a spotting scope come into play from a high point to pick out a trophy head. The stalk is planned, and guide and hunter set off. Although the animal has a poor nose, his hearing is good and his eyesight is phenomenal. As is the case with many other wild animals, a stationary object does not usually scare him away, but if he sees movement and then spots a human being, he'll be out of range in a flash. In order to stay out of sight on a stalk, many hunters have gone ten or twelve miles over some of the roughest country in the world to get within range when the sheep was only half a mile from the starting point. Accurate shooting at 450 or even 500 yards is sometimes needed to take a sheep if he settles down in an open area, but sometimes the hunter can get within 35 or 40 yards if he plans his stalk carefully enough and resists the temptation to look over the skyline from time to time to see if the sheep is still there while he is stalking it.

Hunting Sheep with Bow and Arrow

That archers can take sheep is proof positive that it is sometimes possible to get within close range of this wary game animal. Most mountain sheep taken by archers have been killed in remote sections of Alaska and British Columbia with the services of skilled guides. In 1968, however, a lone American bowhunter performed a feat that is perhaps the most astonishing achievement in trophy hunting ever accomplished in the United States. Ray Alt, a resident hunter in Montana, took a magnificent Rocky Mountain bighorn at about 8,500 feet in the Rockies, hunting in a very rugged area without a guide. Alt scouted the territory thoroughly in advance and located a place where sheep feed on open ridges, where high winds had blown the snow away from vegetation. He camped out in the snow at high altitudes for days before he spotted rams. A lone stalk of several miles brought him above the animals and he came down toward them in a heavy fog. At the last moment, the fog cleared and he found himself below a big ram. He killed the animal with three arrows—two hits and a miss. For this extraordinary trophy and still more astonishing feat, Alt won the most recent Pope and Young Club competition in the Rocky Mountain bighorn category, and also the Ishi Award—an Indian arrowhead mounted on a hardwood plaque. The Ishi Award is the highest award for any kind of trophy that the association of bowhunting archers grants. The group keeps records of North American game killed by archers. So far as is known, Alt is the first lone archer to take a Rocky Mountain bighorn of trophy proportions with a bow since the Indians stopped hunting them in that way.

A sheep that senses a hunter spooks, jumps, and climbs. It seems impossible for a big, heavy animal to run where he does. The sheep easily steps off the edge of a cliff and lands on a narrow ledge thirty or forty feet below, only to spring to another the same distance down. The sheep can cover ground in mountain country as fast as a sprinter can run on level ground. The soft, cushioning pads on its feet help, but the sheep's ability to fly over and down high, broken crags is incredible.

How to Get a Mountain Goat Trophy

The mountain goat, by contrast, is a slow-moving animal which climbs the crags more like a human than the seemingly airborne sheep. The goat places his forefeet carefully, tests the solidity of the stone and his ability to grip it, and then pulls himself up or eases his weight downward. By means of this cautious method, the goat may go where sheep cannot, but he goes much more slowly. If you manage to

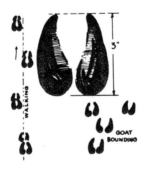

Mountain Goat Tracks

get within camera or rifle range of a mountain goat, haste is unnecessary. He will likely be there for the first shot, the second, and the third. Nevertheless, a mountain-goat trophy is proof that the hunter has climbed high and dangerously for his kill.

The horns of the mountain sheep are very tough and durable. If a sheep takes a hard fall after the shot, the sheep's horns will likely not shatter even after heavy impact on rock. The goat's horns are brittle and shatter easily; therefore the man who shoots a goat should endeavor to anchor the animal so that he cannot roll or jump off a cliff when hit.